CALLING *on the* NAME *of the* LORD

A Journey to Deeper Prayer

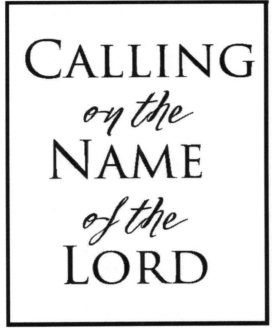

CALLING *on the* NAME *of the* LORD

A Journey to Deeper Prayer

CHAD ROBERTS

Calling on the Name of the Lord

Calling on the Name of the Lord: A Journey to Deeper Prayer

To my parents

Ken & Shirley

You didn't just teach me to follow Jesus, you showed me how by being real, authentic Christians.

Growing up you were amazing parents, but today, you're my best friends.

You have bought me countless books and developed my love for reading. I am so glad to dedicate my first book to you.

Thank you for all you've done. I love you!

CONTENTS

INTRODUCTION

Prayer can be an emotional journey. Have you faced a season where you prayed, yet it seemed God was silent? Worse, have you prayed only to find that life fell apart the more you cried out to God for help? Those can be lonely and difficult seasons.

What does a Christian do when heaven is silent? How do you respond to God when it seems He is not responding to you? My goal in writing this book is to tackle some difficult subjects about prayer and highlight how some of the greatest prayer warriors in the Bible responded to God.

This book will teach you how to pray through difficult seasons. You will learn how Moses faced the pressure of the Red Sea and how he led Israel to trust the promises of God. You will discover how Hannah changed how she prayed after years of praying for the same request. You will see what made her prayer different. You will also learn from King David, Joshua, Blind Bartimaeus, and others.

Together, we will learn how to call on the name of the Lord by following Biblical examples.

Because the Bible shows us beautiful glimpses into people's prayer lives, it can shape the way we think about and practice prayer.

I will share my experiences in this book to show how the Bible has shaped my own prayer life. I do not want to be someone who talks about prayer yet rarely prays. Instead, I want to be that person Paul describes in 1 Thessalonians 5:17 who prays "without ceasing."

How does one get to the place where you are continuously in prayer? I believe it is by growing our sensitivity to the Holy Spirit and how He leads us. When I am aware and more dependent on the Holy Spirit in my daily living, my prayer life is going to naturally grow and mature.

I must invite the Holy Spirit into my praying. If I don't, my prayers will be based on my own strength and my own guidance. I cannot afford that because my strength is small and my understanding is limited. When I invite the Holy Spirit into my praying, I can have His help. It is then His strength that is sustaining me and it is His counsel that is guiding me. Can you see the difference? Are you praying in the power of the Holy Spirit and making decisions in your life with His guidance and help?

Jude 1:21 instructs us, "But you, beloved, building yourselves up in your most holy faith and praying in the Holy Spirit." If I am going to fulfill this command, then I must learn how to pray with the help and guidance of the Holy Spirit.

This book is designed to grow our dependence on the Lord. Out of a greater dependence on Him comes a strong and more active prayer life. So often our prayers are self-centered. It was in 2007 that God began to show me how prideful my prayers were. I found the teachings of John Piper at that time, and they had a big influence on my life. I heard him say, "A fish doesn't know it is wet because all it knows is water." He went on to explain how self-centered and arrogant we can be with God. So many times we do not see it because all we know is arrogance.

The Lord used that to show me how self-centered I was in prayer and how I was not as submitted to His will as I once thought.

The Bible teaches in Romans that we should trust the Holy Spirit to help us pray. Read this carefully: "Likewise the Spirit helps us in our weakness. For we do not know what to pray for as we ought, but the Spirit himself intercedes for us with groanings too deep for words. And he who searches hearts knows what is the mind of the Spirit because the Spirit intercedes for the saints according to the will of God. And we know that for those who love God all things work together for good, for those who are called according to his purpose" (Romans 8:25-28).

Can you say that your prayer life resembles Romans 8? Rather than praying for our usual requests in the normal way, what if we asked the Holy Spirit to lead us and invited Him to teach us what and for whom we ought to pray? That is what this book is about—learning to pray through the power and guidance of the Holy Spirit. The more we lean on the Holy Spirit's guidance, the more we will find ourselves praying for the right things, in the right way, and for the right purposes. Thank you for taking this journey with me as we learn together how to call on the name of the Lord.

Chapter One
The Day I Called Upon the Lord

I had waited all winter for the Sunday of March 1, 2015. Not only would the coming spring bring warmer weather, but I knew the sermon series, God Is Able, would trigger new excitement and momentum within our church. We had spent months preparing both sermons and songs. We were so pumped about this series, we even developed spring T-shirts around our theme. I knew in my heart that this was an important season for Preaching Christ Church.

What I did not know was how God would use my personal life and my family as the main sermon illustration. I had prepared a strong sermon to launch the new series. I was no more than fifteen minutes into preaching it when I saw a flurry of activity in the back of the church, which was very unusual. I saw fifteen to twenty people come from the nursery and kids' church hallway. I saw practically all of our staff, deacon, and elder teams come from the office area. I knew instantly that something was wrong. Danny Walker, our student pastor, slowly approached my podium. My first thought was that a medical emergency had taken place in our kids' church wing. He whispered in my ear, "Your dad is in the ER and you have to leave right now. They don't think he is going to make it." My first reaction was to pray. Even before I left, I wanted to pray. I told the church what Danny had just said, and the entire congregation came forward to pray with me. It was a short drive to the ER. Chad Darnell, a deacon at Preaching Christ Church, and Buddy Capps, my father-in-law, rushed me to the hospital. By the time I got there, my father had crashed and it seemed there was little hope. The ER staff were doing all they could to keep him alive. That evening, the doctors decided to put him on life support. They told us to brace ourselves because they did not think he would survive the night. I remember it being the longest day of my life.

Death Has Never Been So Close

I have done so many funerals. I have walked with countless families through death, yet death had never been this close to me. I could feel it, and I did not know how to pray. Part of me wanted to intercede and cry out to the Lord for Him to spare my dad's life. Part of me knew how exhausted and tired my dad was, and I knew that if he passed from this life into eternity, it would be the greatest day of his life. I was torn. I was tired. I was overwhelmed. Around 2:00 p.m., I went down to the hospital chapel. I was hoping no one would be there. I was surprised when I walked into the small room. It was empty, but it didn't feel empty. I could sense the presence of the Lord there. I got on my knees and poured my heart out to the Lord. I told Him everything. I told him how scared I was and all that was in my heart. When I had finished praying, I couldn't believe how the Lord was ministering to me. From the moment I got the news my dad was dying, I had not felt alone one single moment. The Lord was with me. I did not realize how near He was until that moment.

He began to show me that if He is indeed my Shepherd and I am His sheep, then He was leading me. I was walking the path He knew was good for me. Even if He was walking me through the valley of the shadow of death, I was to fear no evil because He was with me. That day in the hospital chapel, His rod and His staff comforted me. I got so close to my Shepherd in those moments. I experienced Psalm 34:18, "The Lord is near to the brokenhearted and saves the crushed in spirit." I could feel Him being "a very present help in trouble" (Psalm 46:1). That night, things went from bad to worse. I could not believe how raw my emotions felt. I was trying to trust God. I was trying to be realistic and prepare my heart if Dad passed. One moment I would soar in faith and the next moment I was thinking how I would explain to my four-year-old and two-year-old that papaw was in heaven. I couldn't imagine how it would feel when they would ask for him and he was not there. Around 4:00 a.m., the nurse came into the waiting room to tell me they thought my dad had experienced a series of seizures. The entire situation felt hopeless. The next morning, I could tell the doctors were surprised he'd survived the night. I remember asking the primary doctor, "What do we want to see today? What would be a win?" He looked at me with no hope in his eyes and said, "Chad, your dad is as sick as a human being can possibly be." Pneumonia had turned septic in his blood.

Exhausted from being up all night, I went home to try to sleep. I couldn't. Many of you have been there. You know the emotions. You know the overwhelming exhaustion. I began to weep and cry out to the Lord. I got on my knees and prayed with an intensity and an earnestness like never before. While I was praying for God to touch my dad, I was also trying to prepare my heart for his passing.

Before the Throne of Grace

I went back to the hospital that afternoon. When I went into the critical care unit to see my dad, I knew in my heart what I needed to do. I asked everyone to leave me alone with him. I took his hand and I brought us before the Lord according to Hebrews 4:16, "Let us then with confidence draw near to the throne of grace that we may receive mercy and find grace to help in time of need." I didn't just pray. I called upon the Lord. I didn't just ask the Lord for help. I cried out to the Lord with all my heart. It felt as though I had no tears left, but hot tears kept coming, falling onto his arm. I called on the Lord to do His will and to do what glorified Him most. I asked the Lord to do what was good for my dad and my family. When I was finished, I knew something had happened. I didn't know what. I wasn't sure if he would walk out of the hospital or if my dad would soon walk onto the shores of heaven. But as I turned to go out of his room, hearing behind me the life support machine breathing for him, I knew in my spirit that God had heard me and that something was happening. I could feel His grace over my family and our horrible situation.

That night was just as long and just as difficult as the one before. The next morning, I asked the doctor, "What would be a win for today?" Again, not much hope. Around 3:00 p.m. that afternoon, the nurses came to get us and were in complete shock. Something had awakened my dad and somehow he got his hands free and physically pulled the life support tubes out of his mouth. They were astonished. I couldn't believe it. God had touched him in a miraculous way. After a few more days, his strength returned and my dad left that hospital by the power of God and to the glory of God.

A Watershed Moment

This was a watershed moment for my faith. It changed the way I prayed. It changed the way I trust in the Lord. God used this to deepen and fortify my faith. I do not think it was the healing that strengthened my faith. Even if things had not worked out the way I had hoped and the Lord had seen fit to take my dad that day from this earth into heaven, I believe this experience still would have deepened and strengthened my faith and prayers.

One of the greatest lessons the Lord taught me through this experience was what we find in Mark 11:22. Jesus told His followers, "Have faith in God." I pondered this so deeply during my dad's illness. What did it mean to have faith in God? The Holy Spirit really ministered to me from this phrase in the Bible. He showed me that to have faith in God did not mean to have faith in my prayers or in the outcome. Having faith in God is not the same as having faith that God is going to do what I'm praying for or even hoping for. No! To have faith in God means that you trust His plans, even when they hurt. You trust God's decisions, even when it's painful. I settled in my soul that whatever is to God's glory is ultimately to my good. I walked away from this experience not calling on the Lord to get what I wanted, but looking to Him for the strength to sustain me through such a hard experience. To me, the real miracle is not that my dad survived, although I am immensely grateful that he did. Every birthday, every holiday, every Sunday that I see him walk through the doors of my church, I am deeply thankful. The real miracle is that I found God faithful to His Word. He never left me. He never forsook me. As Paul said in 2 Timothy 4:17, "But the Lord stood by me and strengthened me..."

The Lord was a help to me in my deepest time of trouble. The next time I face a circumstance that is overwhelming, I know from experience that God is able to lead me to a rock that is higher than myself (Psalm 61:2), and I know that I can count on His faithfulness to keep me
through life's fiercest storms.

The Day My Dad Enters Eternity

My dad is still sick. The last time I took him to the doctor, he looked at my dad and said, "Mr. Roberts, you are terminal." As we were leaving, I told my dad, "We are all terminal. Each one of us has an appointed time to die, according to Hebrews 9:27." I cannot fully say how I will feel the day my dad passes from this life into eternity. My hope is that "the peace of God which surpasses all understanding will guard" our "hearts and minds in Christ" (Philippians 4:7). But I do not know exactly how I will feel. What I do know is that it will be the greatest day of his life. For the first time, he will breathe celestial air. For the first time in decades he will suffer no pain and he will experience death for the last time. Jesus said, "I am the resurrection and the life. Whoever believes in me, though he die, yet shall he live" (John 11:25). As Christians, we have a hope. This is why Jesus said, "Let not your hearts be troubled. Believe in God; believe also in me. In my Father's house are many rooms. If it were not so, would I have told you that I go to prepare a place for you? And if I go and prepare a place for you, I will come again and will take you to myself, that where I am you may be also" (John 14:1-3). We still grieve, but our grieving is different from that of the world's (1 Thessalonians 4:13). Because of Christ's accomplished work on the cross and because of the miracle of salvation, we are assured of this great promise, "He will wipe away every tear from their eyes and death shall be no more, neither shall there be mourning, nor crying, nor pain anymore..." (Revelation 21:4).

Chapter Two
PRAYER: A Beautiful Exchange

"And call upon me in the day of trouble; I will deliver you and you shall glorify me." Psalm 50:15

There is a beautiful exchange that happens when we pray. Unfortunately, not everyone sees the real meaning of prayer and so it becomes mundane, routine, and for most, nonexistent. Ask ten people what prayer means to them and you will get ten different answers. Without the guidance of Scripture, we are left to ourselves to understand and practice prayer. My goal is to help you discover the Biblical way we should be praying. If left to myself, my prayers can become self-centered, focusing solely on my needs and wants, and this is not what prayer is intended to be.

Thankfully, the Bible does not leave us to ourselves in describing or defining prayer. Rather, it carefully teaches us how to approach God with the right attitude and the right motive. When we get serious about following the Lord, we will have the same desire the disciples had in Luke 1:11, "Now Jesus was praying in a certain place, and when he finished, one of his disciples said to him, 'Lord, teach us to pray...'"

It is fascinating to me that the disciples never asked Jesus how to teach parables. Nor did they ask Him how to perform miracles. Rather, they asked Him how to pray. We too can learn the right way to approach God. We ask the Lord for things all the time. We ask for better this or more of that, we ask for strength, guidance, and maybe even more faith. But how often have we asked Him to teach us to pray?

As we learn the Biblical reasons God wants us to pray, I hope your confidence and ability to call on His name grows stronger. It is my desire that God would use this resource to cause prayer to become even more meaningful to you.

A 30,000 Foot View

Psalm 50:15 shows us the process of prayer and gives us a 30,000-foot view of what it looks like when we call on the Lord. Read carefully what it says, "And call upon me in the day of trouble, I will deliver you and you shall glorify me."

Before we unpack this verse together, notice a few points we will highlight throughout the text. First, we will see that our responsibility is to call on the name of the Lord. God moves through our prayers. It was Hudson Taylor, the great missionary to China in the late 1800s, who used to say, "When man works, man works; but when man prays, God works." Secondly, God responds to our prayers by delivering us and giving us help in our time of need. Lastly, we respond to God's help by glorifying His name. In this, we find the beautiful exchange in prayer. We cry out to the Lord, He delivers us, and we glorify Him. That is quite an exchange!

The Wrong Way to Pray

Prayer should not be a wish list nor a list of demands. I have seen well-meaning Christians believe they can hold God hostage by quoting Bible verses to Him. They think they can "bind God to His Word." This is not a Biblical way to pray nor is it spiritually healthy. Why would I want to bind God to His Word when I do not know what is best for me?

Jesus teaches about God's desire to be good to His children in Matthew 7:9-11 when He remarks, "Or which one of you if his son asks him for bread, will give him a stone? Or if he asks for a fish, will give him a serpent? If you then, who are evil, know how to give good gifts to your children, how much more will your Father who is in heaven give good things to those who ask him!" I do not have to doubt God's goodness or be fearful over His plans for my life.

What I learn from Matthew 7 is that I can trust the Lord. I don't have to manipulate God's plan to somehow work in my favor. No! According to Romans 8:28, "All things work together for good, for those who are called according to his purpose." Furthermore, God assures me in Jeremiah 29:11-13, "'For I know the plans I have for you,' declares the Lord, 'plans for welfare and not for evil, to give you a future and a hope. Then you will call upon me and come and pray to me, and I will hear you. You will seek me and find me when you seek me with all your heart.'" If I really believe that verse of Scripture, I know that ultimately God is working every situation out for my good and that when I pray, I find the heart of God.

I find it very special that the Lord says, "When you seek me with all your heart." I connect this phrase with God's desire for me to trust Him and the plans He has for me. I'm so glad that God cares about the matters of our hearts. He understands our emotions. So often the struggles we have with the Lord are issues of our heart. No wonder Proverbs 4:23 says, "Keep thy heart with all diligence, for out of it are the issues of life" (KJV).

Are there areas of your life where you are not trusting God? Perhaps you are trying to find the answers or you are trying to work the angles to make things come together. What would happen if you put more energy into prayer and trusting the Lord than into trying to do things on your own? I find a world of comfort in how the Bible teaches me to trust in the Lord with all my heart.

And Call Upon Me

What does it mean to call on the Lord? Several years ago when I was a young pastor, I was unmarried and did not have a spouse to talk to and pray things out with. I remember a big need coming into my life, so I called some people I knew would pray for me. I made phone call after phone call until, eventually, I did not have anyone else to call. I remember sitting there thinking to myself, "Who else could I call?"

It was as if the Holy Spirit nudged my heart and said, "Chad, what about Me? You are calling everyone you know to pray for you and not once have you prayed!" I was embarrassed when I realized what I had done.

It is easy to call on other people for help. We seek advice, encouragement, and even strength from everyone but God. Have you ever stopped to consider how this must offend the Holy Spirit?

God has given us His Spirit to be a help and comfort. John 14:16 describes His work. Notice how the verse says, "And I will ask the Father, and he will give you another Helper, to be with you forever, even the Spirit of truth, whom the world cannot receive, because it neither sees him nor knows him. You know him, for he dwells with you and will be in you."

The Holy Spirit is there to help us and guide us. If He is our "Helper" as John 14:16 describes, how much it must grieve Him when we need the Lord's help but we do not pray as the Bible teaches us. Many of us are guilty of treating prayer as a spare tire. We are glad it is there, but we hope we do not have to use it. Surely this offends God!

I think the Biblical idea of calling on the name of the Lord shows God our great need and dependency on Him. Bible teacher and author A.W. Pink wrote, "Prayer is not so much an act as it is an attitude – an attitude of dependency."

Is your attitude one of self-reliance and self-sufficiency? If so, you may be sinning! Look what Jeremiah 2:13 says, "My people have committed two sins; they have forsaken me, the spring of living water, and have dug their own cisterns, broken cisterns that can hold no water." We were never designed to be self-sufficient. If you are a

Christian but relying on your own abilities, you may be sinning in the eyes of the Lord.

I'll never forget a man who came into the place where my mother-in-law works. He had just purchased a new car. She said something to the effect of, "God has blessed you with a nice car." Do you know how he responded? He said, "God did not give me that car. I worked for that car and I purchased it." How foolish! That is a great example of being self-sufficient. Sadly, that man does not understand that it is God who gives him the health to work, the opportunity to earn income, and the ability to even drive.

How well do you feel your need for Jesus? You may make a great deal of money. You may be in good health and you may have the warmest and caring family, but even in the midst of such blessings, we should still sense our need for the Lord. When we call on His name, we are displaying an attitude of dependence upon Him and this is deeply glorifying to God.

The Day of Trouble

There are many days of trouble and it is important to know where to go when we face them. Nahum 1:7 reminds us, "The Lord is good, a stronghold in the day of trouble; he knows those who take refuge in him." What a beautiful promise from the Lord. God is a stronghold for us and we can take refuge in Him."

Where do you go when you face seasons of hardship? For some, the day of trouble is living with bouts of depression. For others, the day of trouble is dealing with a chronic illness, a wayward son or daughter, or perhaps an addiction that you cannot seem to overcome.

The verse from Nahum makes me think of Proverbs 18:10, "The name of the Lord is a strong tower; the righteous man runs into it and is safe." Do you know what these verses are saying to us? We do not have to face life alone! If you are in the middle of a severe storm, if crisis has hit your life, then you need to run to Jesus! He is the strong tower! He is our refuge. In Him, you will find strength, safety, and shelter.

I Will Deliver You

"I will deliver you" is a powerful statement in God's Word. You should memorize it and repeat it over and over. God has a remarkable track record of delivering His people. Everywhere you look in the Bible we see God actively delivering those who call upon Him. We see it from the Red Sea and the children of Israel to Daniel in the lion's den to Peter walking out of prison as the gates opened themselves.

All over God's Word are His great acts of deliverance. You know, God is active in our day as well. The Bible says in Hebrews 13:8 that God is the same "yesterday, today, and forever." Isaiah 59:1 (NIV) says, "Surely the arm of the Lord is not too short to save, nor his ear too dull to hear."

God is able and He has the know-how to deliver us out of any situation or circumstance life throws at us. Your confidence should not be in yourself or in others. Your confidence should be in the Lord and His ability to deliver when we call upon Him.

And You Shall Glorify Me

Now we have come to the most important phrase of this verse. In this, we find a beautiful exchange of prayer. Initially, we call upon the Lord for help. Then He comes to deliver us and helps us in our time of need. Now what is our response to His help? We glorify Him! What a beautiful exchange prayer is!

God is glorified when our prayer life moves beyond routine words, foolish demands, and never-ending wish lists. When prayer becomes a heart reflecting our deep need for Jesus, this is when we will see the Lord working in our daily lives. As Christ followers, we look back to see His faithfulness and we look ahead trusting in His sovereign plans. It is my prayer that faith and confidence will grow in your heart for your joy and God's glory.

"After they had eaten and drunk in Shiloh, Hannah rose. Now Eli the priest was sitting on the seat beside the doorpost of the temple of the LORD. She was deeply distressed and prayed to the LORD and wept bitterly. And she vowed a vow and said, 'O LORD of hosts, if you will indeed look on the affliction of your servant and remember me and not forget your servant, but will give to your servant a son, then I will give him to the LORD all the days of his life, and no razor shall touch his head.' As she continued praying before the LORD, Eli observed her mouth. Hannah was speaking in her heart; only her lips moved, and her voice was not heard. Therefore Eli took her to be a drunken woman. And Eli said to her, 'How long will you go on being drunk? Put your wine away from you.' But Hannah answered, 'No, my lord, I am a woman troubled in spirit. I have drunk neither wine nor strong drink, but I have been pouring out my soul before the LORD. Do not regard your servant as a worthless woman, for all along I have been speaking out of my great anxiety and vexation.' Then Eli answered, 'Go in peace, and the God of Israel grant your petition that you have made to him.' And she said, 'Let your servant find favor in your eyes.' Then the woman went her way and ate, and her face was no longer sad." (1 Samuel 1:9-18)

Chapter Three
OVERWHELMED - Be Anxious for Nothing

Are you someone who struggles with anxiety? Do you often find yourself stressed out? Odds are either you are anxious, or you know someone who is. We want to take the Word of God as medicine in us to handle stress and anxiety. Scripture tells us exactly what to do. And if we will pay attention to the natural logic of Scripture, you and I are going to be far better equipped to handle times of anxiety that come into everyone's life.

Stress in Today's Culture

Stress is a big deal in our culture today. The National Institute of Mental Health tells us that over fifty million Americans feel the effects of some type of anxiety disorder. We battle issues of stress, anxiety, and depression. Perhaps someone you know is afflicted by mental disorder. It prevails within our culture. The National Institute of Mental Health tells us that of all mental disorders, anxiety is number one among women in America. Anxiety is number two among men, second only to drug and alcohol abuse. Mental health is a huge issue for our country.

Why are we so anxious in our culture? Why are we so frantic and panicked? Why are we so stressed and hurried? How do we eliminate anxiety from our lives? What does it mean to slow down and find God's rhythm for your life and not to allow others to set the pace for you? Anxiety has a grip on our society, and perhaps it has a hold of you. We need to use God's Word as the remedy for anxiety. We have to learn how to enjoy unhurried rest, unhurried relationships, and unhurried prayer. We are going to apply these lessons to our culture which is moving at a neck-breaking pace.

The Medication of God's Word

I am not a pastor who rails against doctors and medications. But I do want to share my thoughts very carefully and very pastorally: if you take some type of anti-anxiety medicine, I want you to ask the Lord if this is His will for your life. There are certain, legitimate circumstances which call for medication. I am not against professional medical help; however, I am asking whether you are looking to the help of the Lord, first and foremost. In Philippians chapter four, we are going to find the prescription for obliterating stress and anxiety from our lives.

Following are my questions to those who want to follow Jesus: Are we aware? Are we conscious? Are we actively taking the prescription remedy of God's Word when it comes to our anxiety and stress? At the time of this writing, the most Googled scripture in

America was, "Do not be anxious about anything, but in everything by prayer and supplication with thanksgiving let your requests be made known to God. And the peace of God, which surpasses all understanding, will guard your hearts and your minds in Christ Jesus" (Philippians 4: 6-7). So why as a culture are we not getting it? Because we are missing half the remedy. Verses four and five are just as important as verses six and seven: "Rejoice in the Lord always; again I will say, rejoice. Let your reasonableness be known to everyone. The Lord is at hand." People who are anxious, think anxious thoughts; people who are angry, think angry thoughts; and people who are lustful, think lustful thoughts. Proverbs 23:7 says, "...as a man thinks, so is he" (NKJV). Think on these things: "...whatever is true, whatever is honorable, whatever is just, whatever is pure, whatever is lovely, whatever is commendable, if there is any excellence, if there is anything worthy of praise, think about these things" (Philippians 4:8). We will also learn the meaning of contentment. Paul said, "...I have learned in whatever situation I am to be content. I know how to be brought low, and I know how to abound. In any and every circumstance, I have learned the secret of facing plenty and hunger, abundance and need" (Philippians 4:11-12).

A Closer Look at Philippians 4

If I had a treasure box, an heirloom, a box of priceless gems, how do you think I would handle the box? Do you think I would fling it in the back of my car, throw it around, or thank God haphazardly? No, if I were to own such treasure, I would open it ever so carefully. I would gently handle the gems. In this same careful manner, I present Philippians chapter four, verses four to seven. These words are precious, priceless gems that I want us to carefully unfold and unpack, as we would handle exquisite treasure.

> [4]Rejoice in the Lord always; again I will say, rejoice. [5]Let your reasonableness be known to everyone. The Lord is at hand; [6]do not be anxious about anything, but in everything by prayer and supplication with thanksgiving let your requests be made known to God. [7]And the peace of God, which surpasses all understanding, will guard your hearts and your minds in Christ Jesus (Philippians 4:4-7).

Rejoice... "Rejoice in the Lord, always; again, I will say, Rejoice." It seems Paul asked something quite impossible. How can I rejoice in the Lord in every circumstance? How can I not be anxious about anything? How is that even humanly possible? Do you know what you and I need to realize about Paul when he wrote this letter? His location. He was not at a resort. He was not on a balcony overlooking the Mediterranean Sea, drinking an ice beverage, and enjoying his perfect life. Rather, Paul was in a Roman jail cell, arrested for preaching the Gospel. Paul had been shipwrecked. Paul had been whipped and stoned. Paul had been abandoned and forsaken by his closest friends. Read the whole book of Philippians, the entire letter. Even in Paul's circumstance, even in the dark, cold, damp prison in which he penned these words, Paul was able to say, "Rejoice in the Lord..."

Always... Rejoice, not in your present circumstance, not when it is convenient, not when you are on the mountain top, not when things feel good in your life. Rejoice...Always. Not on certain days of the week, nor certain times of the year... when you get the bonus check, when you land the job, get the promotion... NO! Rejoice in every circumstance. Rejoice in the Lord, always.

As our family was heading out one day, my wife Sadie and I were locking up the house. I went to the back-deck door to lock it first. Then, I walked to the front door and slid the bolt. I exited the house from downstairs, near the car, and I asked Sadie if the door was locked. I clearly asked: "Do-you-have-the-keys?" She did not answer. To be safe, I carefully unlocked the door before I shut it. She then told me, "I got the keys. Go ahead and lock it." So, I walked back again and locked the door. All the while, just guess who did not have the keys? I am currently actively memorizing Rejoice in the Lord. Always. But do you think I rejoiced in the Lord at that moment? Do you think I looked at my wife and said, "Well, you are just the cutest thing." We are the Pastor's Family, and this was a perfect opportunity to practice rejoicing and thanking the Lord. But no, instead, I snipped at Sadie, and she snipped right back at me. Then Emmy, our little six-year-old said, "Are you two in a fight?" Sadie and I had been married for over 10 years, and we had never locked ourselves out of our house. Yet there we sat.

So, we called the locksmith, and there was mad Sadie, sitting in the car. I decided to keep my distance and to sit on the front porch. I did not even want to be beside her. I was sitting there, and as I paused, do you know what God did? He dealt with me. He deals with us all, does He not? I did not want to rejoice, but God reminded me, "Hey Chad, at least it is not hot outside. At least it is the morning. At least it is a Saturday and you do not have an appointment. You are not late for anything. At least you just finished eating breakfast and had something to drink. At least you have the money to pay the locksmith."

Rejoice-in the Lord... "...in the Lord..." means to invite the Lord into your circumstance. It means to invite the Lord into what is happening in the moment and say, "You know what, Lord, this situation is really not as bad as I think." Then, allow God to deal with it. My son, Hudson, that precious little boy, already has a criminal record. He has broken two of our windows and two of our toilets. He flushed a fork down one, and flushed a thin Johnson baby bottle down the other. I had to replace both toilets. He has broken his elbow. And his most notorious act: he broke our flat screen TV. Again I will say, Rejoice... The word rejoice is repeated, as though it were not enough. Paul knew we needed a double exhortation. And again, I say rejoice.

Let your reasonableness be known to everyone... Another word for reasonableness is gentleness. This is my favorite definition of the word. It literally means to have the right attitude. And even more specifically than the right attitude, it means to have a mature attitude. It means to have the right response. As a matter of fact, the opposite of reasonableness is to overreact. Are you someone who overreacts? Reasonableness means to approach a problem without overreacting. How do you find yourself reacting in difficult, trying circumstances? Do you find yourself rejoicing in the Lord always? If you and I can follow the very logical and spiritual steps of verses four and five, the outcome is going to be verses six and seven. But often instead of responding biblically, we search Google for stress remedies. Sometimes we will even search for a Scripture verse remedy (maybe the ever-popular "anxious for nothing" Google verse search). Then somehow we think we will react correctly. Faulty thinking occurs because we are only taking half the remedy. The real prescription is to "Rejoice in the Lord, always" (at all times, in all seasons, and all circumstances). If you are single, rejoice in the Lord. If you are married, rejoice in the Lord. If your marriage is struggling, rejoice in the Lord. If you are widowed, rejoice in the Lord. If you are unemployed, rejoice in the Lord. If your days are difficult; if you are unable to pay your bills; if it feels like you are never going to see the light at the end of the tunnel; if you are facing illness--- Rejoice in the Lord, always. And as you rejoice in the Lord, your reaction will create reasonableness. It is going to create the gentleness, the right attitude, and the right response; so when life throws you a curveball; when the rug gets pulled out from under you; when you smack into a brick wall; when you get blindsided--- you are going to have the right response. People will take notice and say, "I do not know how she is handling that." They will look straight past you, and they will see the hand of God that is in your life.

Do not overreact. Have a mature way of thinking. We take our frustrations out on the ones we love the most, do we not? I do an enormous amount of counseling, and I have sat with people who have told me, "I just blow up for a minute. I do explode, but then it is over." I want to reply, "A tornado only lasts a few seconds; an earthquake lasts only a moment; but look at the damage they leave behind." My friend, do not excuse your overreactions. They are not of God. And the damage caused by emotional outbursts to our children; the damage to our spouse; the damage to our co-workers; the damage to the testimony and grace of the Lord, Jesus Christ...the damage can be irreparable. Do not excuse overreactions. The Bible teaches us to let our reasonableness, to let our attitudes, to let our right responses-let it be seen by everyone. You are a new creation in Christ. Old things have passed away, and all things have become new (II Corinthians 5:17). Receive that medicine in Jesus' name. Amen.

The Lord is at hand... To me, the most important phrase of this chapter is at the end of verse 5: "...The Lord is at hand." However, the chapter and verse numberings do not emphasize the importance of that statement. When Paul and others wrote the text of the Bible, they did not write in chapters and verses. Those additions were made centuries later. I thank God that the Bible is now broken into chapters and verses because it helps us memorize and study. It helps us know where we are in the Word. Can you imagine how difficult it would be to study the Bible as one long letter, without verse numbering and references? You have to understand that when Paul was writing, he was not numbering verses, so the importance of surrounding phrases can easily be lost. Too often, we try to understand a verse from only a snippet of information, which might make the verse seem impossible to obey until we realize the full context. For example, consider verse six: "do not be anxious about anything..." Let us go deeper into the text. What is the foundation of "Do not be anxious about anything"? It is found in this little phrase: "The Lord is at hand." Some translations say, "The Lord is near." In other words, God is with you. As Hebrews 13:5 teaches, "[God] will never leave you nor forsake you." God is with us. He is near us. He is helping us, so why should we be anxious? Why should we worry or fret or be concerned about anything that crosses our path in life? God is with us, His presence, His promise; He is in the midst of our circumstances. That is the basis. That is the foundation of recognizing and understanding the meaning of this verse.

Excuses

We are not to be stressed out. Stress and anxiety are not the will of God for our lives. Do not accept them. Do not say, "Well, my mom was this way. Oh, my dad was that way. I have been this way my whole life." No, do not accept stress! It is not God's will. Why? Because God is right there, doing life with you. God is right there helping you. Now, let me prove it to you. Follow the logic. Because God is near us, we will rejoice in the Lord, always. And again, I say rejoice. Invite him into every circumstance. We are going to rejoice- not in what we are facing, not in our struggle, not in how we are feeling- we are going to rejoice in the Lord. No matter how we feel, we rejoice in the Lord as He continues to lead us in whatever path He chooses.

Emotions: Our Gauge, Not Our Guide

It is a mistake for us to be led by our emotions. Do you realize God gave us our emotions simply as a gauge not as a guide? Does your gas gauge tell you where to go? No. That is the job of your GPS. The gas gauge just tells you when your tank is full or when it is low. In the same way, the emotions that God has given you are not to guide your life. Emotions are not to direct your decisions. If I feel angry, the purpose of the emotion is to tell me how I feel. I am to pray, "God help me with this anger." I may feel sad, lonely, depressed, bitter, or jealous.... I experience many emotions, but they are not to tell me what to do. Emotions simply serve as my gauge, not my guide. And when I am low, I need to be filled with the Holy Spirit. I need to say to God, "Lord, I am not supposed to feel this way. I am going to rejoice right now in You, not in what I feel." So follow the logic: If I rejoice in the Lord always, then my thinking is going to be affected. My attitude is going to be affected. I am going to have the right response. I am not going to overreact. I am going to have reasonableness that everyone sees. And because the Lord is at hand, and I have invited him into the circumstance in my life, then why should I be anxious?

Some days the Lord helps me get so much done, that as I accomplish my tasks. I am at peace. But then there are also moments when I hit a brick wall, figuratively. And there are moments when fret, worry, and anxiety creep up behind me; so I did not even see them coming. How am I going to respond? What am I going to do when an emotion creeps up from behind and surprises me? The Bible tells us, "Do not be anxious about anything, but in everything by prayer and supplication with thanksgiving, let your requests be made known to God" (Philippians 4:6). Let's dig into this idea to better understand what Paul is trying to teach us. Is Paul talking about a blanket prayer? No. He is talking about a very specific kind of prayer.

Four Categories of Prayer

There are four categories of prayer. For each category, do a self-assessment and ask: Am I engaged in all four areas of prayer?

Worship and Adoration. First base is prayer. In the original Greek, prayer means worship and adoration unto the Lord. Yet we often pray with blanketed, general statements: "Oh God, help me in this, help me in that. And God, if You could give me this, and Lord, please make that work..." This type of prayer to God is simply a wish-list that never goes into the other categories. Instead, Jesus taught us to pray, "...Hallowed be Thy name"(KJV, Matthew 6:9). The book of Psalms teaches us truths like the following: "Oh God, there is none like You. You know the help that I need. But, before I even ask for that help, Lord, I want to exalt You. I want to tell You, God, that I believe You are sovereign. I know You control all things. I know there is nothing too difficult for You. God, I look to Your greatness and power. There is none like You, Lord." Sadly, as we pray, we tend to go right into the problem: "Well, God, I do not even know if You are listening. I do not know if You can do anything. God, I do not even know if You can help me." The drastic difference in our manner of praying is clear. God does not want us to approach Him with a wish-list. He wants us to approach Him in the awareness of Who He is, in adoration and worship.

Supplication. The second category is supplication. What is supplication? It is exactly what it sounds like it is. We are the supplicant, which has the idea of humility. In other words, I am not in a position to demand of God. The Lord is our Shepherd, and we are His sheep. Do you think sheep know what they are doing? Sheep rely on the shepherd. As His sheep, we come humbly to God and say, "God, because You are so great, because You are so powerful, because You are so loving and gracious, because Your mercies are renewed every day, because Your love for me is so consistent.... O Eternal God, based on Your glory, greatness, and goodness, I submit all to You. You are the Potter. I am the clay. Make my heart and mind soft like clay. Make my thinking and my will ever so soft, so that You can shape and form me. Oh God, remove the rough edges from me. If You have to make me uncomfortable by removing things out of my life... if You have to change my attitude...if You have to walk me through trials, valleys, or hardship- God, do whatever You must to make me into your image." That is a prayer of supplication. Try it. Pray, "I do not know what is good since I am a sheep. But God, You know what is good; therefore, I submit to You in humility." Anxiety has no power when you pray in this manner.

Thanksgiving. Have you ever baked something and left out an ingredient? Do not miss the ingredient of thanksgiving, the third category of prayer. As I consider my prayer life, how much thanksgiving have I sprinkled into my prayers? "God, You know what I am wrestling with. God, You know what I need right now, but beyond that, I want to thank You for all You have done. Thank You for Your grace. Thank You for the ways You have helped me. I can look back on my path and know You have helped me here. You have helped me there. And here and there." Thanksgiving should be as much a part of our praying as worship and supplications in humility. We need to consider whether thanksgiving is the significant part of our prayer life that it needs to be.

Again, prayer is worship and adoration. It is supplication as shown in humility. (He is the Potter. We are the clay.) Thanksgiving leads us to rejoice in the Lord. As we rejoice in the Lord, we are going to be able to be thankful in prayer. See how it all ties together?

Specific Requests. After you have accomplished all of the above, then, "...let your requests be made known to God." Make your request. What does request mean exactly? Request means specific praying. When you pray to God, do you pray specifically? Recently, I had a meeting that I was dreading. I knew that this person did not see eye to eye with me on everything. So before I sat down at the meeting, I did not just pray, "God bless the meeting and help me." No. Instead, I prayed specifically. I said, "God, will You soften this person's heart? Will You soften my heart? Even though we do not see eye to eye, will You help us get on the same page? Will You help us find points of agreement? God, will you help us relate to one another? And will you give favor and grace?" See what a difference praying specifically makes? God invites you to pray specifically. God invites us to worship and to pray prayers of humility, not just to pray general, blanket prayers. He invites us. He invites us to pray prayers of thanksgiving. He invites us to pray very pointed, specific prayers. Praise God.

Consider the Logic

The Lord is at hand. Because the Lord is at hand, I am not going to be anxious about anything. And why am I not anxious about anything? I am not anxious about anything because I am learning how to pray. I am praying adoration prayers. I am praying humility prayers. I am praying thanksgiving prayers. I am praying specific prayers. And Paul says in verse seven, "And the peace of God, which surpasses all understanding will guard your hearts and your minds in Christ Jesus." Let us understand this verse. It has been well said that the pathway to peace is paved with prayer. Can we say, "Amen!"? You will get peace no other way except through prayer. And that is why the devil does not want you to pray. But the more you pray the correct, biblical way, the more peace you will experience. Then peace will battle and will replace anxiety and stress in your life.

The peace of God...The greatest definition I know of peace is not the absence of problems. Peace is not the absence of trouble. Some of us are being strangled with troublesome thoughts. Sometimes there are legitimate fears which are not always bad. I want my kids to be afraid of the road, right? I want them to fear running out into the middle of the street because a car could hit them.

I want them to fear the hot oven or the hot stove. There are some things that are good to fear. Fear sees a legitimate problem and warns me, "I had better not do this." But do you know the difference between fear and anxiety? While fear sees an actual problem, anxiety only imagines a problem. How many things have you and I worried about in life that have never happened? And yet we worry, and we fret, and it takes our energy and our peace. Prayer will pave the way to a path for peace in your life. Peace is not the absence of problems; rather, peace is the presence of God in the midst of problems. You see the difference? God has not given us His great grace to go around problems in our lives; instead, God has given us His grace to go through them. You can have the peace of God through every problem of your life.

One Big Thing

I do a tremendous amount of marriage counseling, and when I sit down with a couple in trouble, often in their minds, there is "one big thing" that is the source of their problem. It is one mistake. It is one disaster. It is one miscommunication. But relationship concerns are not resolved by addressing just "one big thing." Even if we fix this one thing, there are going to be a hundred other problems to follow which cause tension and miscommunication. It is not one thing troubling you. Your focus must adjust. You might say, "If I could just get that job, if I could just marry that person, or if I could just leave that person. If just this one thing would work out." No, no, no.

Peace (true, biblical, godly peace) is not the absence of trouble. it is the presence of God in the midst of trouble.

And the Bible says that the peace of God is so valuable that it surpasses all worth. It surpasses all wisdom and knowledge. It literally surpasses our understanding. We cannot wrap our minds around the peace of God. It is that valuable. How much money do you have? You still can't buy peace. I do not care how intelligent or creative you are. I do not care what your lot in life is. You do not have the ability to buy, nor to earn, the invaluable peace of God. Peace is priceless, as a rare ruby. And do you know how peace comes? By rejoicing in the Lord, having the right response, and the right attitude. Peace comes by realizing the Lord is near you, He is helping you, and you do not have to be anxious.

I know God's medicine. I do not have to be anxious. I can slam the door shut on anxiety. Why? Because God is near me. And because God is near me, what do I do when I feel anxious? I pray. I bring my adoration, my supplications, my thanksgivings, and my specific requests before God.

Our Umpire

Guard... "And the peace of God, which surpasses all understanding, will guard your hearts and your minds in Christ Jesus." What does the word guard mean in Greek? It literally means umpire. An umpire says, "This is out. This is safe. This is a strike. This is a foul. This is out of bounds." The peace of God will umpire. You may be making decisions that you are anxious over. Do you know why you

43

are anxious? You are anxious because your peace has been violated. There is no peace in you.

God has given you peace to know His will. And when a decision in your life steals your peace, it is not the will of God. God's will is for you to know what to do. In my life, when I do not know how to pray, so often I will ask myself, "Does this situation take my peace? Do I have peace about this?" Why? Because the peace of God will tell me what is right. It will tell me what is wrong. The peace of God will tell me what is healthy or unhealthy in my life. Maybe you are stressed and anxious because you do not have peace in your life. How do you get that peace? Pray the right kind of prayer, and the peace of God will guard. It will umpire. It will call the shots and keep your heart. If you find yourself wishing you could numb your emotions, because you do not know how to feel...my friend, the peace of God will guard your emotions and affections. Maybe you do not even know how to think or what to do. The peace of God will guard your heart and mind in Christ Jesus.

The Safest Place in the Universe

When I consider my affections and my thinking, I want to put them in the safest place in the universe. Do you know where that is? It is in Christ Jesus. Whatever you fret over, whatever you are anxious about, whatever you are troubled by, whatever worries you—each is a result of your thinking. Are your thoughts and feelings in Christ? If they are not, that is the reason you are not experiencing peace. If you will bring your thinking and feeling into Christ, God will give you His peace. And that would be better than my giving you a priceless emerald, ruby, diamond, or sapphire. You can have the peace of God. I do not know your circumstances. I do not know your lot in life, nor your season in life. I do not know the pressure you are under; however, I know God's Word can be as effective in you as it is in me. Will you receive God's Word?

Chapter Four
Taking Hold of God

"But I have been pouring out my soul before the Lord." 1 Samuel 1:15

Hannah is one of my favorite Biblical characters. I can appreciate how the Bible gives few details about a person's life. However, what it does record tells us a great deal about their faith and background. Hannah is a good example of this. She was broken because she wanted a son, but the Lord had closed her womb. The Bible tells us that she prayed year after year, yet it seemed as if God was ignoring her.

As we explore Hannah's life and how she responded to God in her time of desperation, we learn how we should approach the Lord for our own needs. Hannah's prayer is one of the most beautiful prayers recorded in the Bible. In studying her prayer, I believe we will discover how we too can experience breakthrough praying.

Exactly what is breakthrough prayer? I believe it is a place where our praying transcends panic, worry, or doubt. There is a peace that comes into our hearts knowing that God has heard our request and help is on the way. Psalm 57:3 assures those who follow the Lord that He will give us help from heaven itself.

In this chapter, I hope to show you what breakthrough prayer looks like. I want you to see in Hannah's story the sovereignty of God. I also want you to see that, when we face seasons of unanswered prayer, the Lord is not ignoring us. Rather, God is working His plans and part of those plans involve moving us to action like He did Hannah.

Hannah's Home Life

Hannah was married to a good man named Elkanah. The early verses of 1 Samuel 1 tell us that he was a spiritual man, as he would go worship the Lord each year following their customs. I'm sure he was concerned with pleasing the Lord. Verse 5 tells us Elkanah genuinely loved Hannah. He would give her double portions when they would go sacrifice for worship. Despite his great love for her, he failed to understand his wife's feelings.

She had a desire for a child of her own, especially a son. In verse 8 he asked, "Hannah, why do you weep? And why do you not eat? And why is your heart sad? Am I not more to you than ten sons?" I suppose that was a dumb question on his part!

To make matters worse, there was Elkanah's second wife, Peninnah. Because Hannah could not have children, he married a second wife to give him children. You can imagine the tension this caused in the home.

While verse 7 tells us that Hannah was barren "year after year," according to verse 4, Peninnah had "many sons and daughters." Verse 6 explains that Peninnah was Hannah's rival and that she "used to provoke her grievously to irritate her."

Seeing God's Sovereignty

The entire key to understanding 1 Samuel 1, as well as to understanding the purpose behind our own unanswered prayers, is found in verses 5 and 6. Back to back the Bible tells us that "the Lord had closed her womb."

This is the most important phrase in chapter 1 because it tells us the backstory to what is happening. I wonder how many times Hannah thought, what is wrong with my body that I cannot have children? Is there something wrong with me? Since Elkanah had many children with Peninnah, the problem was not with him, it was with Hannah.

How often did Hannah feel like a failure? How difficult were mornings when the children would wake up and run all over the house? What were family dinners like? While I bet it was tense, I'm sure Hannah was the bigger person. I imagine that she still cared for the kids, loved them, and was a part of their lives, even though she was grieving because she could not have any children of her own.

I'm convinced that when Christians recognize God's sovereignty, it deepens and increases our faith like nothing else. I have experienced this in my own walk with the Lord. However, when we fail to see God's sovereignty, it frustrates our faith and causes tension. This affects how we pray, how we view God, and how we respond to life's challenges. When a Christian gets sovereignty straight, everything else straightens out from there.

Seeing God's sovereignty will do two things for you. First, it will eliminate a great deal of frustration. You and I have the benefit of reading the backstory of Hannah's life. We can see that it was God who closed her womb. Scripture confirms that it is the Lord who is working within our own lives, even when it seems to frustrate or hinder our plans. Seeing and acknowledging God's sovereignty removes frustration because you can trust that God is at work, even when you do not see it. Like the old saying goes, "When you cannot see God's hand, you can always trust His heart."

Second, it will move you to action. To find grace and help in our time of need, we must approach the throne of God! How often do we neglect to bring our needs before the Lord? How often do we approach God in a wrong way? I believe the Lord allows us to come to a breaking point where we completely surrender our plans over to Him. This is exactly what happened to Hannah and it moved her to active prayer by calling on the name of the Lord.

Consider what God Is Doing

Ecclesiastes 7:13-14, "Consider the work of God: who can make straight what he has made crooked? In the day of prosperity be joyful, and in the day of adversity consider: God has made the one as well as the other..."

These verses have been an anchor for my soul. When I face seasons of doubt or discouragement, I can go to Ecclesiastes 7 and see that God has made joyful and prosperous days, as well as hard and difficult days. What is the point? The point is that God is working both for my good (Romans 8:28). God's plan is at work, even if it is taking years to unfold. I can trust the sovereign plans of God. "Trust in the Lord with all your heart, and do not lean upon your own understanding" (Proverbs 3:5).

Hannah Pours Out Her Soul

Have you ever poured out your soul to the Lord? Have you prayed from the deepest places of your heart? When I think about Hannah's life, I cannot image the hundreds of prayers she must have prayed for a son. Out of all the times she prayed, what made this one different? As we examine her prayer, I want us to discover what breakthrough prayer is in our own praying? How do we take hold of God and pray in the right way? Here is how Hannah prayed.

A Sincere Prayer

She approached the Lord out of sincerity. She came to Him with a heavy and broken heart. She did not come trying to manipulate God or negotiate. Verse 10 says she came "deeply distressed and prayed to the Lord and wept bitterly." Also verse 16 tells us she prayed out of her "great anxiety and vexation."

In other words, this wasn't prayer as usual. She was brokenhearted. Do you know why it is good to come to the Lord brokenhearted? Because Psalm 34:18 says, "The Lord is near to the brokenhearted and saves the crushed in spirit." Psalm 147:3 goes even further by saying, "He heals the brokenhearted and binds up their wounds."

Satan will try to tell you that you have to have everything together before you can approach God. The enemy will try to get us to spend all of our energy trying to solve our own problems and find the solutions. But in reality, the Bible encourages us to approach God, especially when we are brokenhearted like Hannah.

Hebrews 4:16 says, "Let us then with confidence draw near to the throne of grace, that we may receive mercy and find grace to help in time of need." When I read a Scripture like this, I ask myself why I try to do life apart from the Lord's help. Why would I try to go on in my own strength when the Lord stands ready to help me?

Verses 12 and 13 tell us that as she continued to pray, "Eli (the priest) observed her mouth. Hannah was speaking in her heart; only her lips moved, and her voice was not heard."

John Bunyan, author of the classic *The Pilgrim's Progress*, once said, "In prayer it is better to have a heart without words than words without heart." Psalm 51:17 sums it up by stating, "The sacrifices of God are a broken spirit; a broken and contrite heart, O God, you will not despise." So, are you comfortable coming to the Lord broken? Do you somehow feel like you have to get your life together before you can really pray and call on His name? Allow these Scriptures to minister to your broken heart. Healing the brokenhearted is what the Lord does best!

A Submissive Prayer

Read carefully how Hannah approached the Lord. First it says she "vowed a vow." This was her surrender point. I don't think vowing a vow means she negotiated or bargained with God. I think it means this is the place where she gave her all to the Lord.

Perhaps the Lord knew that if He had given her a son two years or five years prior to this, she may have never given him back to the Lord, and Israel would have never had Samuel, whom they desperately needed. I believe the Lord drove her to a place of surrender.

Could this be why your prayer has not been answered yet? Would you love the answer to your prayer more than you love the Lord? Maybe Samuel would have become Hannah's idol if the Lord had answered this request a few years back? I believe the Lord led Hannah to a beautiful place of surrender and that is how she experienced breakthrough prayer.

Verse 11 goes on to say, "O Lord of hosts." What a tremendous title for the Lord! The Bible uses this title for God over three hundred times. It means the captain of heavenly armies. Hannah is saying, "Lord, will you fight for me? Will you overcome for me?" You should attach this title for the Lord in your own praying.

She then asked the Lord, "If you will indeed look on the affliction of your servant and remember me and not forget your servant, but will give to your servant a son..." Three times she calls herself the Lord's "servant." Do you approach the Lord with this type of humility? Think about it, do we pray so that the Lord can serve us and grant all of our wishes and demands, or are we more concerned with serving His purposes and glorifying His name?

A Sacrificial Prayer

Hannah makes a vow to the Lord and promises to give her son back to God. The end of verse 11 says, "Then I will give him to the Lord all the days of his life, and no razor shall touch his head." In other words, he would be set apart for the service of God.

The Lord Remembers Her

According to verse 19, Hannah and Elkanah went to worship the Lord early the next morning. After they arrived home from their journey, the Bible says that Elkanah "knew Hannah his wife." We probably don't need any commentary to understand what that means. But listen to the next phrase: "And the Lord remembered her." Isn't that wonderful? It's so specific to what she prayed and asked the Lord for! Do you remember in verse 11 when she asked the Lord, "If you will indeed look on the affliction of your servant and remember me and not forget your servant..."? How special that verse 19 says, "...and the Lord remembered her."

May I remind you, child of God, that He knows exactly who you are and where in life you are at this moment? Yes, the Lord knows us! Isaiah 43:1 says, "...Fear not, for I have redeemed you; I have called you by name, you are mine."

I'm so glad the Lord allows us these glimpses into people's lives from the Old Testament. We have seen Hannah struggle year after year and we have seen her rival provoke and irritate her. Finally she goes to the house of God and calls upon the Lord in a special way. She knows she prayed a breakthrough prayer because, according to verse 18, her countenance changed.

Now, the chapter concludes with verse 20 saying, "And in due time Hannah conceived and bore a son, and she called his name Samuel, for she said, 'I have asked for him from the Lord.'"

What do you need from God? Have you approached Him in a way that you are not negotiating or manipulating His plans? Instead, are you looking to the sovereignty of God and trusting His wisdom and counsel for your life? Are you calling on the Lord in a way that is special to you and the Lord? I want to experience breakthrough prayers like Hannah. Not so that I necessarily get what I want, but so that God can tune my heart to what He wants and so my desires become aligned to his will.

When this happens, we can experience the confidence that comes from trusting in the Lord. We can experience His help and guidance, and we can experience the joy of taking hold of God through breakthrough prayer.

Then the LORD said to Moses, "Tell the people of Israel to turn back and encamp in front of Pi-hahiroth, between Migdol and the sea, in front of Baal-zephon; you shall encamp facing it, by the sea. For Pharaoh will say of the people of Israel, 'They are wandering in the land; the wilderness has shut them in.' And I will harden

Pharaoh's heart, and he will pursue them, and I will get glory over Pharaoh and all his host, and the Egyptians shall know that I am the LORD." And they did so. When the king of Egypt was told that the people had fled, the minds of Pharaoh and his servants were changed toward the people, and they said, "What is this we have done, that we have let Israel go from serving us?" So he made ready his chariot and took his army with him. He took six hundred chosen chariots and all the other chariots of Egypt with officers over all of them. And the LORD hardened the heart of Pharaoh king of Egypt, and he pursued the people of Israel while the people of Israel were going out defiantly. The Egyptians pursued them, all Pharaoh's horses and chariots and his horsemen and his army, and overtook them encamped at the sea, by Pi-hahiroth, in front of Baal-zephon.

"When Pharaoh drew near, the people of Israel lifted up their eyes, and behold, the Egyptians were marching after them, and they feared greatly. And the people of Israel cried out to the LORD. They said to Moses, 'Is it because there are no graves in Egypt that you have taken us away to die in the wilderness? What have you done to us in bringing us out of Egypt? Is not this what we said to you in Egypt: "Leave us alone that we may serve the Egyptians?" For it would have been better for us to serve the Egyptians than to die in the wilderness.' And Moses said to the people, 'Fear not, stand firm, and see the salvation of the LORD, which he will work for you today. For the Egyptians whom you see today, you shall never see again. The LORD will fight for you, and you have only to be silent.'" (Exodus 14:1-14)

Chapter Five
The Lord Will Fight for You

"Fear not, stand firm, and see the salvation of the Lord, which he will work for you today." Exodus 14:13

I saw the Red Sea for the first time in 2007. I love the Middle East and have traveled through quite a bit of it preaching the gospel and encouraging churches in countries dominated by Islam, repressive governments, and persecution. On this particular visit, I was traveling through Kuwait, Lebanon, United Arab Emirates, Egypt, and Qatar during a three-week mission. I would fly back to Cairo between speaking opportunities because it was the base of my Middle East operations.

Because this particular trip was long and exhausting, my ministry friends in Egypt arranged a special getaway at a resort on the Red Sea. I'll never forget walking to the shores and being stunned by its vastness. I am not sure what I was expecting, but its size overwhelmed me. The very first thought I had was Israel crossing the mighty sea on dry ground!

God Set Israel Up

What if I told you the Lord pinned Israel between the Red Sea and Pharaoh's army? What would you think if the entire situation was set up by God? This is exactly how Exodus 14:1-4 describes the event. It was the Lord who instructed Moses to encamp Israel between the mountains and the sea. It was the Lord who hardened Pharaoh's heart to pursue the children of Israel, and it was the Lord who had a way of escape.

The crossing of the Red Sea is one of the most thrilling stories of the Bible. As we work our way through these verses of Exodus 14, we understand why God will sometimes pin our own lives between a rock and a hard place. We will see why God hardens some hearts around us and why God seems to bring us to the brink of disaster only to do a great miracle in our lives that gives Him the greater glory.

Gripped with Fear

At this point, Israel has watched the Lord perform quite a number of miraculous events. Not only did they have a front-row seat to the ten plagues of Egypt described in Exodus 7-10, but God is now guiding them with a pillar of cloud by day and a pillar of fire by night. At this point they have made their way through the wilderness, up to the place of the Red Sea. Who among them could doubt God was with them every step of the way? Each time they looked up they would see the pillar of cloud or pillar of fire. Would that not scream to the Israelites that God is with them and helping them?

Before we go any further with the Israelites, let us pause to consider that the Lord has also given us great gifts in our day to assure our hearts that He is with us, leading and guiding our lives. He has given us His Holy Spirit and His Word. What wonderful gifts from the Lord! We need them both to live effective, godly lives.

Many of us have wished that God would speak to us like He did in the Bible. How much easier would decisions be if God wrote on walls like He did for Daniel, or if He would send fire down like He did for Elijah or even if He calmed the seas like He did on Galilee? May I show you something interesting? God's way of speaking to us is through His Word and His Spirit. Peter, who walked with Jesus through some of the most miraculous events to ever take place on the earth, calls Scripture "a sure word" or a "confirmed word" in 2 Peter 1:19. Think about that. Peter heard the audible voice of the Father on the Mount of Transfiguration, yet he calls the Bible a more "sure word."

My mentor in the faith, Terry Whitson, has always told me that I need both the Spirit and the Word. "If you have the Spirit and not the Word, you will blow up. If you have the Word without the Spirit, you will dry up; but if you have the Spirit and the Word together, you will grow up." Is that not a wonderful way to compliment both the Spirit of God and the Word of God?

Let's get back to the Israelites. Picture the scene in your mind. The Red Sea is before them, the mountains are to the side of them, and the wilderness is behind them. There is nowhere they can go. I'm sure Moses was probably meeting with the brightest minds of the one million plus Israelites who had come out of Egypt. All of a sudden they see a cloud of dust coming from the wilderness. I wonder if they could even feel a shaking in the ground. Either way, it struck fear into the Israelites. Let's look at verse 10, "When Pharaoh drew near, the people of Israel lifted up their eyes, and behold, the Egyptians were marching after them, and they feared greatly. And the people of Israel cried out to the Lord."

Now this was not just a platoon coming after the Israelites. It was the entire Egyptian army. Verse 9 tells us, "The Egyptians pursued them, all Pharaoh's horses and chariots and his horsemen and his army." I'm sure this was the scariest thing the Israelites had ever seen, and that is saying a great deal since they had lived through the ten plagues of Egypt!

Are You Kidding Me?

I had always misunderstood this next phrase until I studied it more carefully. The end of verse 10 says, "...and the people of Israel cried out to the Lord." I don't know why, but I always pictured people calling on the Lord in great faith to help them and deliver them.

When you read the verse carefully you find out that is not what happened at all. When the people cried out, they did so out of fear and unbelief. Look at how they responded to Moses in verses 11-12, "Is it because there are no graves in Egypt that you have taken us away to die in the wilderness? What have you done to us in bringing us out of Egypt? Is not this what we said to you in Egypt: 'Leave us alone that we may serve the Egyptians'? For it would have been better for us to serve the Egyptians than to die in the wilderness."

You have got to be kidding me! This is not what they said in Egypt. As a matter of fact, the Bible records how they cried out for deliverance. "Then the Lord said, 'I have surely seen the affliction of my people who are in Egypt and have heard their cry because of their taskmasters. I know their sufferings'" (Exodus 3:7).

So the Lord sent Moses to deliver His people. Now they find themselves in the wilderness facing imminent death. Who do they blame? Moses! But if you notice, it is not Moses who is leading Israel. It is the Lord. He has orchestrated all of the events leading up to the miracle of Israel crossing the Red Sea. Realizing that it was God who was responsible for leading them into this situation gives me tremendous hope and confidence that God also knows what He is doing in my life. When He leads me into difficult circumstances, I don't need to blame others or even myself. I need to look to the hand of the Lord and consider what He is doing in my life.

Fear Not, Stand Firm, See the Salvation of the Lord

The Bible says in Numbers 12:3 that Moses was one of the humblest men to ever live. How he handled the children of Israel at the crossing of the Red Sea shows us why he was an outstanding leader and a godly man.

Rather than resigning his position or throwing the naysayers into the Red Sea (which would have been my first two options), Moses calms the people and reassures them of God's ability to deliver them.

What gave Moses such faith? I wonder if his mind went back to the burning bush experience where God assured him of his calling. Perhaps his mind flashed back to when God caused his staff to become a serpent in Pharaoh's court, displaying God's power and sovereignty over the Egyptian gods. Maybe he simply looked up and saw the pillar of fire and knew God was with him.

Either way, Moses was confident in God's ability to rescue His people. The Bible records him saying in Exodus 14:13-14, "And Moses said to the people, 'Fear not, stand firm, and see the salvation of the Lord, which he will work for you today. For the Egyptians whom you see today, you shall never see again. The Lord will fight for you, and you have only to be silent.'"

I bet they thought Moses had lost his mind. This was an impossible situation. How could they escape the coming Egyptian army? There was no place to hide and nowhere to run. They were literally pinned in. Luke 18:27 says, "What is impossible with man is possible with God." Do you believe this for your own life?

You may be in a situation right now that has you feeling pinned in with no way to escape. It may be a looming bankruptcy or financial catastrophe. It may be a terminal illness where the doctors have told you there is nothing more they can do. It could be a spouse who has walked away, leaving you to pick up the shattered pieces. There are many circumstances in life that pin us in.

I believe the Word of the Lord would say to you what Moses said to Israel. Fear not! Do not be afraid of the future because God is always at work in our lives. We do not know what tomorrow holds, but the Lord does. If our Shepherd leads us down paths that seem scary and frightening, rest assured that He goes before us and that means he has already walked those same paths. Even then, God says they are good for us. Our Shepherd is not behind us pushing us into unknown territory. No! He is ahead of us, leading us, bidding us to come and follow Him! Moses said to the people, "Stand firm." What did he mean by that? It means to stand in the confidence of the Lord. Do not back down. Do not stop praying. Do not stop calling on the name of the Lord! Stand firm in the confidence that the Lord can deliver you and turn your situation for good.

Then he says, "See the salvation of the Lord...the Lord will fight for you...you only have to be silent." Those are comforting words to a frightened heart. Are you looking for the salvation of the Lord? Are you being silent or are you trying to defend yourself and getting swept away with strife, tension, and arguments? No! Let the Lord fight for you. Let Him bring the victory.

The Egyptians You Will See No More

This is probably my favorite phrase of the entire chapter: "For the Egyptians whom you see today, you shall never see again."

I pray that people will see this kind of deliverance in their own lives. I pray that those who are trapped in an affair will never see that affair again. Those who are bound by drug addictions will never see themselves strung out and slaves to it again. Those who are held captive to lust, anger, bitterness, and greed will never see them again. Oh, that God would work in our lives in such a way! Galatians 5:1

instructs us, "For freedom Christ has set us free; stand firm therefore, and do not submit again to a yoke of slavery."

Yes, Christ can set us free from the bondages of sin, but it is our responsibility to "stand firm" in that freedom and to not submit again to the yoke of slavery to sin. Are you standing firm in what God has done for you or do you allow sin back into your heart and even your home? You need to resolve to stand firm in the work God has done in you.

Just as Israel saw the Egyptian army marching to capture them once again into slavery, many of you reading this fear the same. The Lord has delivered you, but deep down you fear that bondage is coming again. Fear not! Stand firm and see the salvation of the Lord. He will fight for you!

Going Forward

The next verse is probably the most shocking to me. After Moses gave this stirring speech and calmed the people down, he then went to God for the game plan. How God responded to him astounds me. Read verse 15, "The Lord said to Moses, 'Why do you cry to me?'" The Bible does not tell us what Moses said to the Lord or even the way in which he said it, but apparently, the Lord was not pleased.

I admit, I wrestled with this. Here Moses is hanging on for dear life. His people are about to die, they are trapped by the mountains, wilderness, and sea, and now Pharaoh is closing in at a rapid pace. When Moses goes to the Lord, God's response is, "Why do you cry out to me?" That seems harsh and unloving to me.

But the Lord went on to say, "Tell the people of Israel to go forward." Unbelievable! God was not going to allow His people to sit in pity. He had too much love for them. He was not going to coddle them and soothe their fears. He said, "Go forward."

Sometimes we need the Lord to calm us and sometimes we need the Lord to simply say, "Go forward." The Lord is not going to allow you to just sit and sulk. If He is going to do a great miracle in your life, it is going to require you going forward in faith. So the point is to not let your feelings get hurt if the Lord is pushing you forward. Trust Him because God always has a plan to work in our lives.

I Will Get Glory Out of Pharaoh

You can read Exodus 14 to see how the Lord parted the waters and Israel crossed on dry ground. The Lord sent an angel to go before them. The pillars of fire lit up the night sky until all of Israel (approximately one million people) had crossed.

When the Egyptian's realized that God was with the Israelites, they said, "Let us flee from before Israel, for the Lord fights for them against the Egyptians" (Exodus 14:25). But it was too late. The Lord hardened Pharaoh's heart to pursue Israel across the Red Sea. When they did, the Lord sent the angel behind Israel and closed the waters on the Egyptian army.

Listen to how this miraculous story concludes. "Thus the Lord saved Israel that day from the hand of the Egyptians, and Israel saw the Egyptians dead on the seashore. Israel saw the great power that the Lord used against the Egyptians, so the people feared the

Lord, and they believed in the Lord and in his servant Moses" (Exodus 14:30-31).

God will work in your life. He will fight for you. What is your responsibility? Fear not. Stand firm and see the salvation of the Lord. In other words, trust in the Lord with all your heart.

"If it had not been the LORD who was on our side— let Israel now say— if it had not been the LORD who was on our side when people rose up against us, then they would have swallowed us up alive, when their anger was kindled against us; then the flood would have swept us away, the torrent would have gone over us; then over us would have gone the raging waters. Blessed be the LORD, who has not given us as prey to their teeth! We have escaped like a bird from the snare of the fowlers; the snare is broken, and we have escaped! Our help is in the name of the LORD, who made heaven and earth." (Psalm 124:1-8)

Chapter Six

If It Had Not Been the Lord
Who Was on Our Side

"Our help is in the name of the Lord, Who made heaven and earth."
Psalm 124:8

Psalm 124 is a special chapter in the Bible for me. Certain phrases in the chapter have a way of stirring my affections for God. King David writes, "If it had not been the Lord who was on our side," "Blessed be the Lord," and "Our help is in the name of the Lord." These marvelous statements about God increase my faith and lead me in deeper prayer and worship.

Our Response

What is interesting about this Psalm is that it requires a vocal response. In the English language, if we want to emphasize what is being said, we end a statement with an exclamation point or we write in all caps to give it importance. In Hebrew, the original language of the Old Testament, emphasis is added by repeating phrases.

To give this phrase even more weight, the Israelites were to repeat it aloud. "If it had not been the Lord who was on our side—let Israel now say—if it had not been the Lord who was on our side..." I think there is something to be said here about becoming vocal in prayer.

I believe things happen when we speak God's Word over our lives. For example, the Bible teaches in Proverbs 18:21, "Death and life are in the power of the tongue, and those who love it will eat of its fruit." The New Living Translation renders this verse as, "The tongue can bring death or life; those who love to talk will reap the consequences." This is a good translation of its meaning.

The way I interpret this for my life is that I am going to be intentional about the things I say. I am not going to go around saying things like, "Everyone in my family has had cancer so I am probably going to get it too." No! I am not going to say things like this! I am going to say that I trust the Lord with my health, and I am dependent on Him and His grace to help me, despite a negative family medical history. The Lord can help me and I am trusting Him.

So does that mean I am fearful over everything I say? No, but it does mean I am aware of what I am saying. It means I am intentional about speaking good, godly, and Biblical things over my life. If I am facing an illness, this is how I am going to pray. I will confess Psalm 118:17, "I shall not die, but I shall live, and recount the deeds of the LORD" and Romans 8:11, "If the Spirit of him who raised Jesus from the dead dwells in you, he who raised Christ Jesus from the dead will also give life to your mortal bodies through his Spirit who dwells in you." This is what I mean by "speaking" the Word of God over your life.

Jesus teaches us how we should handle this in Mark 11:22-24, "And Jesus answered them, 'Have faith in God. Truly, I say to you, whoever says to this mountain, 'Be taken up and thrown into the sea,' and does not doubt in his heart, but believes that what he says will come to pass, it will be done for him. Therefore, I tell you, whatever you ask in prayer, believe that you have received it, and it will be yours.'" Did you notice how Jesus links speaking with praying? You speak to the mountain to be removed when you pray. Mountains in the Bible refer to difficulties. There is great value added to prayer when you become vocal and speak God's Word and truth over your life and family.

Now do not misunderstand what I am saying. I am not indicating that there is "magic" in our words or that we are miniature gods able to accomplish supernatural things just because we say a certain prayer. We are not God. As stated in previous chapters, it is unwise and unbiblical to think we can manipulate God's plans for our lives. But the Bible does teach that the things we say matter. The words we speak over our lives have serious consequences. Ultimately, it is the plans of the Lord that prevail according to Proverbs 19:21, but we have a responsibility to guard the things we say.

The point is that God has given sovereign ability to the words we speak. If you go around saying things like, "I'll always be alone," or "I'll probably die at an early age" or "I'll never get over depression," you may "reap the consequences" because "life and death are in the power of the tongue."

I think that is why it is important to memorize and quote Scripture. There is great power in speaking God's living Word over our lives. Do not be caught saying negative things when God's Word, combined with the power of faith, can move mountains.

Our Enemy

What would Satan do to your life if he could? Think of the devastation he would cause to your family and faith if God allowed it? David vividly describes the desire of the enemies of Israel. He says, "When people rose up against us, then they would have swallowed us up alive, when their anger was kindled against us."

The enemies we face are not like David's. Our enemies are much worse! Our enemies are not physical, they are spiritual. Paul teaches in Ephesians 6:12, "For we do not wrestle against flesh and blood, but against the rulers, against the authorities, against the cosmic powers over this present darkness, against the spiritual forces of evil in the heavenly places."

Jesus modeled this type of spiritual warfare when He looked at Peter and said, "Get thee behind me, Satan" (Matthew 16:23 (KJV)). Obviously, Jesus was not calling Peter Satan. He was simply recognizing the type of thinking influenced by the enemy.

While Paul teaches about "rulers" and "authorities" and "cosmic powers in this present darkness," he also teaches that Christ completely conquered these same "powers" on the cross. Colossians 2:15 states, "He disarmed the rulers and authorities and put them to open shame, by triumphing over them in him."

This is why it is important to live in the power and presence of Christ. There cannot be spiritual triumph in our own strength, cleverness, or strategy. Victory can only be found in Christ! "But thanks be to God, who in Christ always leads us in triumphal procession..." (2 Corinthians 2:14).

Trials and Temptations

The Psalm now transitions from the danger of people to the danger of trials and temptations. The Psalmist writes, "Then the flood would have swept us away, the torrent would have gone over us; then over us would have gone the raging waters."

Commentators believe David was referencing the deliverance of Israel at the Red Sea from Pharaoh and Egypt's army, but we can all probably recall a time in our lives when circumstances nearly drowned us. Perhaps at this moment you are in a situation where you feel like you are drowning. You can draw great hope from this verse. It is the Lord who saves and delivers us!

Think over the promise in Isaiah 43:2, "When you pass through the waters, I will be with you; and through the rivers, they shall not overwhelm you; when you walk through the fire you shall not be burned and the flame shall not consume you." You can call upon the Lord's faithfulness and stand firmly on these promises.

Yes, the Lord promises protection for His people. Countless times we can see God's protection throughout the Bible. No doubt, you can see His protection throughout your life as well. Many of you should not have lived through the wreck you experienced. Some should not have recovered from their illness, and some should not have survived the accident. Time and time again, we can see the Lord faithful to protect His people.

How can we be confident of this? Because if you are born again, you are God's child! 1 John 1:3 says, "See what kind of love the Father has given to us that we should be called children of God, and so we are." Did you notice how this verse does not say that we will one day be children of God? No! It tells us that we are His children now! What assurance!

David knew exactly what he was talking about when he wrote Psalm 77:16, "When the waters saw you, O God, when the waters saw you, they were afraid; indeed, the deep waters." What "deep waters" are you facing right now? Remind yourself of this verse. Can you see what an arsenal of weapons the Bible gives us for times when we are frightened or overwhelmed? Is it any wonder Satan wants to keep us from God's Word?

Do you remember what Jesus said to the Sea of Galilee? The Scripture says, "And when he awoke and rebuked the wind and said to the sea, 'Peace! Be still!' And the wind ceased, and was a great calm" (Mark 4:39). Once again, Jesus links speaking with praying. Don't forget, child of God, the wind and sea still know His name!

Blessed Be the Lord

It is as if David is recalling God's great ability to save and rescue us and cannot help but rejoice by exclaiming, "Blessed be the Lord." What praise will come out of our own heart and mouth when you recall all the times God has helped you and provided for you? Are you able to say, "Blessed be the name of the Lord"?

Do you know when it is most appropriate to bless the Lord? It is not when you are comfortable and satisfied. David tells us in Psalm 34:1-3, "I will bless the Lord at all times; his praise shall continually be in my mouth. My soul makes its boast in the Lord; let the humble hear and be glad. Oh, magnify the Lord with me, and let us exalt his name together!" We are not to only bless the Lord in the good times, but we are to bless Him at all times. It does not matter if you are in a place of great blessing or a season of great trial, you have the ability to bless the Lord exactly where you are.

At this point, David shows how God delivers his people from temptation by saying, "Who has not given us as prey to their teeth! We have escaped like a bird from the snare of the fowlers; the snare is broken; and we have escaped!"

Both Psalm 91 and Psalm 124 assure us God will deliver us from the snare of the fowler, but Psalm 124 takes it even further when we see David celebrating that the snare is broken! This is a good place to ask if the snare has been broken in your life. Perhaps the Lord has delivered you from a sin of your past, but from time to time it resurfaces. You love the Lord and you want to serve Him, but it seems like this certain sin has a grip on your life. The author of Hebrews says it like this, "Therefore, since we are surrounded by so great a cloud of witnesses, let us also lay aside every weight, and sin which clings so closely, and let us run with endurance the race that is set before us."

Is there a sin that clings closely to you? You need the power of God to break the snare of sin. Christ has the ability to break it. The next time temptation rears its ugly head you need to be armed with Psalm 124:7 which says, "The snare is broken; and we have escaped!"

Our Help Is in the Name of the Lord

There is great peace in knowing where our help comes from. How much energy do we exert trying to help ourselves or find others to help, when all we really need to do is call upon the Lord?

People often ask me how they can learn to pray more effectively. I always respond by telling them to pray the book of Psalms. David knew how to pray. He was authentic and transparent with the Lord. He was vulnerable and not self-sufficient. I have learned how to approach God and how to rely more on God by reading, studying, and even mimicking King David's prayers.

One of the aspects I appreciate most about David's prayers is that he relied his entire life on the Lord, whether he was a lowly shepherd boy, a triumphant warrior, or king of Israel. Throughout his entire life we see him calling on the name of the Lord.

David described his confidence in the Lord in Psalm 121:1-2 by stating, "I will lift up my eyes to the hills. From where does my help come? My help comes from the Lord, who made heaven and earth." I hope you are building this same kind of confidence in God's ability to help you.

How Will You Respond?

As you read this, you may be thinking, "I do need the Lord's help, and I need to rely on Him in a greater way. Where do I begin?" I believe as we become more sensitive to our need for the Lord, our desire to pray begins to grow. If you are someone who does not feel a need to pray, then I am sure you do not feel your need for God's help in your life.

The key to growing in prayer is to begin praying the Scriptures. When we read, memorize, and quote the Word of God, we can then access the tremendous power behind it. Indeed, it is "living and active, sharper than any two-edged sword, piercing to the division of soul and of spirit, of joints and of marrow, and discerning the thoughts and intentions of the heart" (Hebrews 4:12).

"So Joshua came upon them suddenly, having marched up all night from Gilgal. And the LORD threw them into a panic before Israel, who struck them with a great blow at Gibeon and chased them by the way of the ascent of Beth-horon and struck them as far as Azekah and Makkedah. And as they fled before Israel, while they were going down the ascent of Beth-horon, the LORD threw down large stones from heaven on them as far as Azekah, and they died. There were more who died because of the hailstones than the sons of Israel killed with the sword. At that time Joshua spoke to the

LORD in the day when the LORD gave the Amorites over to the sons of Israel, and he said in the sight of Israel, 'Sun, stand still at Gibeon, and moon, in the Valley of Aijalon.' And the sun stood still, and the moon stopped, until the nation took vengeance on their enemies. Is this not written in the Book of Jashar? The sun stopped in the midst of heaven and did not hurry to set for about a whole day. There has been no day like it before or since, when the LORD heeded the voice of a man, for the LORD fought for Israel. So Joshua returned, and all Israel with him, to the camp at Gilgal." (Joshua 10:9-15)

Chapter Seven
The Day the Sun Stood Still

"There has been no day like it before or since, when the LORD heeded the voice of a man, for the LORD fought for Israel." Joshua 10:14

There are plenty of people who do not believe in the Bible. They think it is a book of stories and fairytales, often laughing and sneering at its truths. An easy target for those who want to mock God's Word is the Biblical account of when God caused the sun and moon to stand still.

I will tell you why such mocking does not faze me. Not only do I believe God's Word, but I have experienced God's power in my own life. People can argue, debate, and mock all they want, but here is what I know—a man with an experience is never at the mercy of a man with an argument.

For me, Joshua 10 is not about God suspending the laws of nature and causing the sun and moon to stand still. Rather, it is about God's sovereign ability to help His people and fight on their behalf. So if you are someone who doubts whether or not this Biblical account is accurate, I would say that you're missing the entire point. It is not God that you need to try to figure out. It is God's power that you need to experience.

The purpose of this chapter is to learn how to respond when Satan attacks you. There will be times when he launches fierce attacks against your family, your health, or others you love. When those times happen, how do you respond?

Many of you reading this chapter are in need of God working in your life. Joshua 10 should be of great encouragement to you because it shows us God's ability to help us. I invite you to walk with me verse by verse through this exhilarating chapter of the Bible. I pray it encourages your life the way it has my own.

God's Faithfulness

The first ten chapters of Joshua are fast-moving, highlighting the miraculous works of God on Israel's behalf. Just as God walked Israel through the Red Sea on dry ground, He performs yet another miracle in Joshua 3, taking this new generation of Israelites on dry ground through the Jordan River. After the crossing of the Jordan River, Joshua encounters the Lord Himself in Joshua 5, and God gives him the game plan for overthrowing Jericho.

It appears Israel is willing to obey God's commands no matter how ridiculous they may seem. How could they not trust the Lord with what they had just experienced crossing the Jordan River? In Joshua 6, the mighty walls of Jericho come crashing down, and God delivers one of the most monumental victories in Israel's history.

Next, they face Ai. Israel learns a hard lesson as a soldier named Achan sins and causes Israel to lose the battle in Joshua 7. After Joshua deals with Achan's sin, God tells Joshua in chapter 8 to once again battle Ai. God gives Israel their second major conquest in Canaan.

Joshua 5:1 gives us a great overhead picture of what was happening in the land of Canaan when Joshua and Israel entered the land. "As soon as all the kings of the Amorites who were beyond the Jordan to the west, and all the kings of the Canaanites who were by the sea, heard that the LORD had dried up the waters of the Jordan for the people of Israel until they had crossed over, their hearts melted and there was no longer any spirit in them because of the people of Israel."

What an incredible testimony of God's faithfulness to His people. Now that we know some of the backstory of what is happening with Joshua, Israel, and the land of Canaan, we turn our attention to the scene of Joshua 10.

An Unholy Alliance

Adoni-Zedek was the king of Jerusalem. Word must have traveled fast in Canaan because Joshua 10:1 tells us with great detail what is going on: "As soon as Adoni-Zedek, king of Jerusalem, heard how Joshua had captured Ai and had devoted it to destruction, doing to Ai and its king as he had done to Jericho and its king, and how the inhabitants of Gibeon had made peace with Israel and were among them, he feared greatly..."

This king's name is interesting. His name means, "My Lord is Righteous." However, he did not live up to the meaning of his name. He did not have any interest in following the Lord. In a similar way, Lucifer was among the greatest of all of God's creation. His name means "Bright Star." Satan has certainly not lived up to his original name.

Adoni-Zedek forms an alliance with the other Amorite kings and plans to strike before Israel reaches them. Joshua 10:6 says that Adoni-Zedek and the other kings assembled their armies against Gibeon to make "war against it."

A Plea for Help

Gibeon turns to Joshua and Israel in their time of need. Joshua 10:6 says, "And the men of Gibeon sent to Joshua at the camp in Gilgal, saying, 'Do not relax your hand from your servants. Come up to us quickly and save us and help us, for all the kings of the Amorites who dwell in the hill country are gathered against us.'"

In a similar way, the people of this world look to God's people for help. In 2015, I became a chaplain for Trinity Memorial Centers. When families who do not have a pastor experience a death, the funeral home calls me to do the memorial service for the family.

While I enjoy meeting these families, I am aware that they do not have a church nor a pastor in their life they can call on. I often wonder how people make it through such circumstances without a church family who will lift them up to the Lord.

When the people of Gibeon got into trouble, they looked to God's people. When people get in trouble, it should be the Church that they want to turn to.

Recognizing Our Enemy

Just as Israel faced the Hittites, Jebusites, Canaanites, and many other enemies, so we face an enemy. Peter describes him in 1 Peter 1:5, "Be sober-minded; be watchful. Your adversary the devil prowls around like a roaring lion, seeking someone to devour."

Paul teaches us in Ephesians 6:12, "For we do not wrestle against flesh and blood, but against the rulers, against the authorities, against the cosmic powers over this present darkness, against the spiritual forces of evil in the heavenly places."

Do you know why that verse is so important? It is because many of you have loved ones who you get so frustrated with. Their lives are gripped by the power of sin, and it causes you to get mad at them. They are not the enemy! Satan is the enemy. What we fight and struggle against is the spiritual darkness that influences their lives.

The Weapons of Warfare

So how do we fight spiritual darkness? How do we stand in the gap for those we love and pray effectively? Paul teaches us the power of prayer in 2 Corinthians 10:4. Read this verse with great expectation. "For the weapons of our warfare are not of the flesh but have divine power to destroy strongholds." Amazing! Do you see why your prayers are so effective? They have the power to destroy strongholds. No wonder Satan tries to hinder us from praying. I'm disappointed when people posts on social media for prayer and others say silly things like, "Sending good vibes" or "Sending positive thoughts." When I am facing a spiritual attack, I do not need anyone's good vibes or positive thoughts. They do not have the power to break strongholds. What I need are people who know how to pray and get ahold of God. I need people to intercede and call on the name of the Lord on my behalf. Only the power of prayer can destroy strongholds. This is my weapon of choice!

People of War

Joshua 10:7 is one of my favorite verses of this text. It says, "So Joshua went up from Gilgal, he and all the people of war with him and all the mighty men of valor." These are special words to me. As a pastor, I have seen Satan launch fierce attacks against the people of God. It is in these times you need "people of war" and "mighty men of valor."

In the spring of 2016, a family in my church, the Byrds, were experiencing the flu. It went from the dad to both of their boys, and then their thirteen-year-old girl fell ill. They naturally thought she had the flu like the rest of the family had experienced because it was in the same time period.

After a couple of weeks, she was getting worse and they were growing more concerned. They took her to urgent care. After getting examined, she was rushed to the ER. What began from there was a long and fierce battle for her life.

She was admitted to the hospital and was diagnosed with double pneumonia. The doctors could not believe the extent of the pneumonia in her right lung. After five days in the hospital, the doctors were still concerned. They could tell the pneumonia was leaving, but her fever was still at 103. Her bloodstream was also infected. A doctor said he wanted to do a full CT scan of her body on that Thursday morning.

What the doctors discovered was horrific. The pneumonia was so severe in her right lung that it had eaten a hole through her right lung and had begun to leak out into her body. Friday morning they rushed her from Kingsport to the Children's Hospital in Knoxville, TN. I'll never forget the phone call from her dad. He called me around 4:00 p.m. Friday afternoon and said, "Pastor, Grace is in bad shape. She is in critical care. Her right lung is dead and she needs prayer now."

From that moment, I felt as though I experienced Joshua 10. Great friends had reached out to us and asked that we come to their side and call on the Lord. Satan was attacking their family with a fierceness that they needed the "people of war" and "mighty men of valor" to help them. We took to social media and called for prayer. Beginning at 7:00 p.m. Friday night, we established twenty-four hours of prayer for Grace Byrd. For the next twenty-four hours she would have someone before the throne of God calling her name out. What a powerful thought to have someone before the Lord every hour on your behalf.

As a church, we were praying many Scriptures over Grace, but there is one that came to the forefront. Summer Hamrick, our Safety Team Coordinator, had Mark 5:41-42 on her heart and this is the Scripture the people of war began to pray. Read it carefully, "Taking her by the hand he said to her, 'Talitha cumi,' which means, 'Little girl, I say to you, arise.' And immediately the girl got up and began walking (for she was twelve years of age), and they were immediately overcome with amazement."

We knew the Lord's ability to heal Grace. We believed with all our hearts that God could touch her. There was an entire team of doctors working on her from 4:00 p.m. till midnight. Her heart was out of rhythm, her blood pressure was out of control, and her right lung was medically "dead."

I knew in my heart that she was at death's door. I remember praying and reminding the Lord that we have lost precious people from our congregation. Heaven is sweeter with them there. But I did not want to lose Grace. If God, in His sovereign wisdom, chose to take her, as heartbreaking as it would be, we would say as a church, "The Lord gave and the Lord has taken away; blessed be the name of the Lord" in accordance with Job 1:21.

By the grace of God, we have never lost a child. I reminded the Lord how we have lost others and have modeled glorifying God, even in dark and difficult times. I explained how much it would mean to me if He would have grace upon Grace.

All that night, we battled for Grace's life. My wife, Sadie, was at Myrtle Beach attending a women's conference with several other ladies from our church, so I was home with our kids. The next morning, I arranged for my parents to watch my girls while I went to Knoxville to be with the family.

I arrived at the hospital around ten Saturday morning. David, her father, was exhausted. I could see it all over his face, but he had some good news. He said that all through the night she had been near death. Her hands and feet were ice cold. Her nails had even begun to turn purple and blue. He said he had never been so scared in his life. Yet he kept praying that bittersweet prayer so many of us have prayed, "Not my will, but yours be done." What a hard prayer to pray in those situations.

He said around 5:00 a.m., things began to change. All of a sudden her color returned. Her vitals stabilized. Surely the Lord was touching her! I had not been there but about thirty minutes when she began to get very restless. She was on a ventilator and the doctors said she would be sedated for approximately four to seven days. They said it could take anywhere from hours to days for her to wake up and begin talking.

To our astonishment, she awoke before noon that Saturday! They said she would need to go from the vent to a bi-pap machine. She didn't! She went from the vent to breathing on her own. Her right lung began to function and the hole that had been created by the pneumonia had repaired itself.

By 2:00 p.m. Saturday, she was sitting up in her bed, with vitals stable, talking to her family and guests. It was one of the greatest, sweetest miracles I have ever seen. Just hours before, we were in the throes of death and now she was wanting Bojangles to eat! It was absolutely amazing and deeply God glorifying.

It was still a long road to recovery, but God had delivered her and her family from death! She was released from the hospital several days later. It was about a month before she could come back to church, but the Sunday she returned was a great celebration of God's faithfulness.

Like every church, there are plenty of flaws with the church I pastor. You could pick out several areas we need improvement in. However, there is one area I have tremendous confidence in and that is our ability to pray. I have seen it time and time again. Do you have people in your life who will go to war with you? Are you someone who can go to war on behalf of others? I want to surround my life with people who are "mighty men of valor" and who know how to pray and pray effectively.

I thank God for people who know how to call on the Lord and fight back the darkness. I believe with all my heart that the prayers of the saints saved Grace Byrd's life. God was glorified and great joy came to our church as a result.

God Guarantees Our Victory

Do you know what surprises me about this portion of Scripture? God did not promise victory to Joshua before they left to fight. They left by faith! Joshua 10:7 says they went up from Gilgal, then verse 8 tells us what God said to them, "And the Lord said to Joshua, 'Do not fear them, for I have given them into your hands. Not a man of them shall stand before you.'"

Perhaps you're reading this wondering if you will ever experience such victory in your life. You may be thinking, "I've heard stories like this, but I've yet to experience God's power." I would ask you, are you engaged in the fight or are you sitting back waiting to see God do something supernatural? What I learn from Joshua's story is that he engaged in the war before he got the promise of victory. Perhaps the Lord is waiting for you to move and engage before He shows you His power.

It fascinates me that Joshua and the men of war went before God promised the victory. I want to act in that type of faith. I want to be active and willing to wage war against the enemy. Do you realize that God has already promised us the victory over Satan? If Joshua acted this quickly, how much more should you and I be willing to engage in spiritual warfare knowing the promises from Scripture and having the power of prayer and having experienced the power of God?

If you are fighting for your marriage, your children, or on behalf of those you love, think over these promises from the Bible. These Scriptures guarantee us victory over Satan and his plots for our lives. Put these verses to memory and go to war with them. These are our weapons!

"For the LORD your God is he who goes with you to fight for you against your enemies, to give you the victory." - Deuteronomy 20:4

"But thanks be to God, who gives us the victory through our Lord Jesus Christ." - 1 Corinthians 15:57

"No, in all these things we are more than conquerors through him who loved us." - Romans 8:37

"Little children, you are from God and have overcome them, for he who is in you is greater than he who is in the world." - 1 John 4:4
"I can do all things through Christ who strengthens me." - Philippians 4:13

"For sin will have no dominion over you, since you are not under law but under grace." - Romans 6:14

"But thanks be to God, who in Christ always leads us in triumphal procession, and through us spreads the fragrance of the knowledge of him everywhere." - 2 Corinthians 2:14

Our Responsibility

Joshua 10:9 has an interesting phrase. After Joshua and his men had marched all night from Gilgal, and even though the Lord promised them victory in the verse before, notice what Joshua does in verse 9, "So Joshua came upon them suddenly..."

I think this verse is saying that, even though God promises victory, we still have a responsibility to engage in the fight. We cannot sit back and wait for God to work in supernatural ways when we are not willing to do our part.

Is there an area of your life where you need to respond suddenly? It may be someone you need to forgive. You don't need to carry the hurt and bitterness any longer. You should forgive them suddenly. Perhaps you don't financially give to the Lord because you are waiting till you are out of debt or earning more. I would encourage you to obey the Lord suddenly and begin giving.

There are many areas of our lives where we can lag in obedience, whereas God wants to see sudden obedience. God can be faithful to do His part when we are faithful to do our part. Do you think a great victory would have been won if Joshua and his men had half-heartedly engaged in the fight, waiting for God to do something supernatural? I do not think the Lord would have brought such decisive victory if Joshua had not done his part. What is it that the Lord wants you to do? Be quick to do it!

God Gets His Glory

Joshua 10:10-11 gives some details of the battle. While Israel engaged in the fight, it was really the Lord who gave the victory. It says the Lord "threw them into a panic" and then "threw down large stones from heaven." The end of verse 11 makes it clear who won the war: "There were more who died because of the hailstones than the sons of Israel killed with the sword."

God killed more of the enemy with hailstones than Israel could kill with the sword. God will get His victory from your life. We have our part and God has His part.

Joshua's Declaration

I'm amazed at the courage Joshua had to make such a bold, audacious statement. I have to ask myself why Joshua had this much trust in God's divine power. Because of all that he had witnessed the Lord do for Israel. The crossing of the Red Sea and the Jordan River. The victories of Jericho and Ai and how the Lord had appeared before him, giving him confidence that just as He was with Moses, God was with Joshua.

Likewise, the Lord builds our faith as well. We can look back over our lives and see how God was with us in various circumstances. We can recall the faithfulness of God, and it builds our faith for what we face going forward.

Before Joshua commanded the sun and moon to stand still, notice how he first spoke with the Lord. Joshua 10:12 says, "At that time Joshua spoke to the Lord in the day when the Lord gave the

Amorites over to the sons of Israel..." In the midst of the fighting, Joshua was still praying and communicating with the Lord. Often, when we are in the middle of a battle, it can seem overwhelming and, often, we stop praying. It is all we can do to stand and fight, let alone communicate with the Lord. But Joshua made this his priority. In the middle of the war, Joshua is praying and talking to the Lord.

Then being moved by the Spirit of God, Joshua makes this incredible declaration in verse 12, "...And he said in the sight of Israel, 'Sun, stand still at Gibeon, and moon, in the valley of Aijalon.'" Verse 13 says, "And the sun stood still, and the moon stopped, until the nation took vengeance on their enemies."

You Have Fighting to Do

The point of Joshua 10 is that God is fighting with us. When we face times of warfare, God is on our side, and He is engaged in the fight alongside us. This gives hope to our prayers. The story of the sun and moon standing still shows us in a physical way what God wants to do in our spiritual lives as we pray and call on His name.

If God would suspend the laws of nature for His people to win a fierce battle, what will He do for us in the Spirit? How much greater is His ability to break the power of sin? If God can turn the hearts of kings as the rivers, according to Proverbs 21:1, then surely God can turn your loved one's heart toward the Lord! Is anything too hard for God? The account of Joshua 10 answers that question with a resounding NO!

So what do you do while you are praying? Well, you have some fighting to do. You speak to your circumstance. You speak faith to your situation and say, "Stand still in Jesus' name." For example, you may be fighting an illness. Speak to that disease and say, "Stand still." Maybe there is an addict in your life who you are interceding for. Speak to that addiction and say, "Stand still" while you pray to break the power of sin in their life.

But do not forget, long before Joshua made a declaration for the sun and moon to stand still, he was willing to fight. He was already engaged in the battle, and he was in constant prayer with the Lord.

Will the Lord suspend the laws of nature today? No. Joshua 10:14 makes it clear that there has never been another day like this since. So why is it recorded for us? Of what benefit is it to our spiritual lives today? The point is what God did in the physical, He is able to do in the spiritual. This story shows us what God is able to do through prayer. There is a new day God has for you. In between the sun and moon of your situation standing still, you have a war to wage. Fight with the power of God. Fight with the power of prayer and watch the Lord do for you what He did for the sons of Israel on that historical and Biblical day. God will fight for you and He will give you the victory.

"On the third day there was a wedding at Cana in Galilee, and the mother of Jesus was there. Jesus also was invited to the wedding with his disciples. When the wine ran out, the mother of Jesus said to him, 'They have no wine.' And Jesus said to her, 'Woman, what does this have to do with me? My hour has not yet come.' His mother said to the servants, 'Do whatever he tells you.' Now there were six stone water jars there for the Jewish rites of purification, each holding twenty or thirty gallons. Jesus said to the servants, 'Fill the jars with water.' And they filled them up to the brim. And he said to them, 'Now draw some out and take it to the master of the feast.' So they took it. When the master of the feast tasted the water now become wine, and did not know where it came from (though the servants who had drawn the water knew), the master of the feast called the bridegroom and said to him, 'Everyone serves the good wine first, and when people have drunk freely, then the poor wine. But you have kept the good wine until now.' This, the first of his signs, Jesus did at Cana in Galilee, and manifested his glory. And his disciples believed in him. After this he went down to Capernaum, with his mother and his brothers and his disciples, and they stayed there for a few days." (John 2:1-12)

Chapter Eight
What Do You Need?

"His mother said to the servants, 'Do whatever he tells you.'" John 2:5

When Jesus and His disciples accepted an invitation to a wedding, the bride and groom had no idea what a special guest He would be. Weddings are a big deal in our culture, but not like they were in Jesus' culture. Today's weddings may last an hour or so. Jewish weddings typically lasted six to eight days. They were community events and the expectations were sky-high.

So important were the food and wine that if a wedding party ran out, they could legally face a lawsuit. Both the families of the bride and groom would be stigmatized by the culture and feel the weight of the shame for years to come.

A Jewish engagement was actually a contract between the families of the future bride and groom. This was called the betrothal stage. Under Jewish law, they were considered already married. They neither lived together nor consummated the marriage, but they were legally promised to marry.

This is why when Joseph learned that Mary was pregnant with Jesus, he wanted to "divorce" her. In our western culture, we would ask how Joseph could divorce her without consummating their marriage.

The betrothal stage was a difficult period for the couple as it was a lengthy time of separation. Sometimes it lasted over a year. The separation was intended for two primary reasons. First, the groom would learn a new trade or master his life's skill. The time apart allowed him to concentrate on making a living for his new family. Second, he would build what was called a bridal chamber onto his father's house. When the bridal chamber was complete, he was ready to marry his bride.

What a beautiful picture of Christ and His Church. Knowing how the groom went away and prepared a bridal chamber makes John 14:1-3 all the more real when it said, "Let not your hearts be troubled. Believe in God; believe also in me. In my Father's house are many rooms. If it were not so, would I have told you that I go to prepare a place for you? And if I go to prepare a place for you, I will come again and will take you to myself, that where I am you may be also." What a promise! For further study, read Jesus' parable of the ten virgins and the bridegroom in Matthew 25.

Now we understand the seriousness of Jewish weddings, the cultural expectations as well as the legal ramification. We can now begin to understand Mary's urgency and the great need they had when she said to Jesus, "They have no wine" (John 2:3).

We All Have Needs

One of the greatest joys I have as a pastor is the counseling work I do. I love to help people who are overwhelmed with life's hurts. Because God has given me a shepherd's heart, it gives me a deep sense of satisfaction to work with couples or individuals. Sometimes we work for six to eight weeks to discover the roots of their problems and to dig those roots out. It is amazing to see spiritual transformation as we pray and talk together.

However, there is one aspect to counseling that always surprises me. People usually think their problems are unique to their situation. Yet in reality, their circumstances are quite normal. It is typically either communication issues, pride, self-centeredness, or some other inward behavior that leads to the need for counseling.

What happens is we begin to think thoughts like, "If my life were different, life would be better." This is a lie from Satan! Rather than changing our behaviors or attitudes, we think changing spouses, changing jobs, or changing churches will solve the problem. Many people are trapped in cycles because they focus on changing the outward circumstances instead of changing inward behaviors.

The point is, we all have needs. Each of us face struggles, doubts, and fears. There will come seasons in our life when we need God's help and the help of His people to get us through.

I have counseled wealthy people, yet their money could not help them. I have counseled intelligent and analytical people, but they could not see a way out. It does not matter how comfortable life is, how healthy you are, or how smart you are. There will be times when you need to call on the name of the Lord. The purpose of this book is to help you in those times.

John's Remarkable Details

In John 2:2, Jesus and His new disciples are invited to a wedding. There are quite a number of interesting points in the text. The Apostle John, who authored the Gospel of John, the epistles of John (1, 2, and 3), as well as the book of Revelation, helps us as we read the text. He is so vivid in his descriptions that the reader can put themselves there and see the events as they unfold with their mind's eye.

I appreciate the detail with which John writes. His audience is the universal reader, whereas Matthew wrote primarily to a Jewish audience. Most of the details of Matthew are intended for the Jews. That is why Matthew opens his gospel with the genealogy of Jesus. For a Jewish reader, it would prove that Christ is the Messiah. The Gospel of Mark was written to a Roman audience and the Gospel of Luke was written to a Greek audience.

When we understand that John's gospel is intended for a universal audience, is it any wonder that it includes, "For God so loved the world, that he gave his only Son, that whoever believes in him should not perish but have eternal life. For God did not send his Son into the world to condemn the world, but in order that the world might be saved through him. Whoever believes in him is not condemned, but whoever does not believe is condemned already, because he has not believed in the name of the only Son of God" (John 3:16-18).

First, John tells us where this wedding takes place. He says it was at Cana of Galilee. This is an important detail to the student of the Bible. Had John simply said, "Cana," it could have been the Cana of Asher mentioned in Joshua 19:28. The reason why Cana of Galilee matters is because it was a small town approximately five miles northwest of Nazareth. We know Nazareth was the hometown of Jesus. This is where His family was from.

John gives us many small details to indicate that this probably was the wedding party of close friends, perhaps even relatives of Jesus' family. This makes sense with the location being next to Nazareth. Another few indicators are that Jesus, His brothers, and Mary all attended the wedding as a family, according to John 2:12. The obvious question is, where is Mary's husband, Joseph?

Because Jesus asked John to care for His mother after His death (John 19:26), it is most likely that Joseph passed away early in life. For him not to be mentioned in the John 2 account indicates that Joseph had passed before Jesus was baptized by John the Baptist. It is also interesting that John never calls Mary by her name throughout his gospel. He simply refers to her as Jesus' mother (John 2:1; 2:3; 6:42; 19:25). This was most likely a sign of deep respect. While Jesus was invited to the wedding, John tells us Mary was "there." It almost sounds as though she wasn't invited but served from the beginning. Could she have been organizing the food and drinks? It appears she might have been because she stepped in to resolve a serious issue. She also gave orders to the servants and told them to do exactly as Jesus commanded them. It would appear that she had some level of authority within the wedding party.

The Greek word John uses for "servants" in verse 5 is the word diákonos, from which we get our English word "deacon." It simply means to serve. It is not the word used for slaves, which is douleúō. This tells us that the servants Mary directed were most likely family, at the least friends, again, indicating that either the bride or groom were relatives of Christ.

I also find it fascinating that John helps the Gentile reader understand the purpose of the stone pots they filled with water. He explains in verse 6 that there were six stone pots used for the "Jewish rite of purification." The Jews would wash their hands before and after each meal. You would think these large pots would also come in handy for catering situations, as you would need large amounts of water for cooking and cleaning.

When these six stone pots were filled with water, John adds a specific detail in verse 7, saying, "And they filled them up to the brim." Why is this detail important? Because it says nothing was added to the water. It was 100% pure water filled to the brim, totaling nearly one hundred and fifty gallons of water. John tells us these stone pots held nearly twenty to thirty gallons of water each.

Jesus and Mary

Now that we understand the legal and cultural ramifications of running out of wine and the remarkable details John gives to his readers, I want to focus on the relationship between Mary and Jesus. Another puzzling point to John 2 is why Jesus calls His mother, "Woman" in verse 4. He then asks her, "What does this have to do with me?" It leaves the reader in our culture thinking Jesus was being rude to His mother.

The Greek word for woman is the equivalent of our English word, "Ma'am." It is not quite as disrespectful as it seems in our culture. But while calling my own mother "Ma'am" wouldn't seem as disrespectful as calling her "Woman," it would still seem odd. So why did Jesus address Mary this way?

No doubt Mary had heard about Jesus' cousin, John the Baptist, baptizing Him, which is recorded in John 1. This had just happened before the wedding. I bet Mary was so excited that now people would finally see who Jesus was and why He came. Apparently, what she was asking her Son to do was to reveal Himself as the Messiah, because Jesus' response was, "...My hour has not yet come" (verse 4).

Jesus calls His mother "Ma'am" because He is showing her that their relationship is going to change now that He has begun His

99

earthly ministry. When He asks, "What does this have to do with me? My hour has not yet come," He is saying that this is not His real purpose in coming to the earth.

John 13:1 gives us a glimpse into Jesus' real purpose in coming. The verse reads, "When Jesus knew his hour had come to depart this world, he loved his followers to the end."

Mary's Faith

I love Mary's faith. When Jesus said this, she did not argue with Him. She did not try to persuade nor convince Him. She simply looked to the servants in verse 5 and said, "Do whatever he tells you."

I would have loved to have seen Mary in action. I bet she was a real leader. I wonder if she threw her hands up and said, "Jesus, I know you can help this situation. I know you have the answer. Do whatever You have to do!"

I don't want to manipulate God. I don't want to foolishly quote Him Scripture and try to make God do what I want. I want to rely on Him and say, "God, I know You can help me. Do whatever You need to do, Lord. I trust You!"

Spiritual Application #1: Jesus' Invitation

One of the strongest spiritual applications to this text is how Jesus was invited to the wedding. How easy it is to overlook this detail. We should stop and ask ourselves, "Have I invited Jesus into my life? Have I invited Him into my problems? Have I invited Him into my marriage or career or health?" So often we fight life's problems alone.

But Jesus is willing and even eager to help us. Why do we not invite Him into our situation?

If we're going to see God work in our lives in supernatural ways, then we must invite Him into the situations of our lives. James 1:21 is a great example of what our attitude should be toward God and His Word. It says, "Therefore put away all filthiness and rampant wickedness and receive with meekness the implanted word, which is able to save your souls." The Greek word for "receive" is "Dechomai," which literally means to put out a welcome mat.

Is this not an incredible picture of God's Word? When we welcome His thoughts and principles into our lives, then we receive it with open arms. We receive it into our hearts, our minds, and even our homes.

Warren Wiersbe says, "When you receive the Word with meekness, you accept it, do not argue with it, and honor it as the Word of God. You do not try to twist it to conform to your thinking." (Wiersbe, Warren. *Bible Exposition Commentary*. (Wheaton, IL, Victor Books, 1989)).

The point is, if we invite Jesus into our circumstances, that means we invite His Word into our hearts and lives. Are you willing to receive (put out the welcome mat for) God's Word? How different would your problems look if you invited Christ? What would happen to your marriage if Christ were really invited? What would change about your health, finances, or career if Christ had an open invitation to work and move in those areas? The answer may surprise you.

Spiritual Application #2: Do Whatever He Tells You

There is another application to our text that is so simple that we can miss it. Mary's response to the servants in verse 5 is the key to understanding this section of Scripture. She says to the servants, "Do whatever he tells you."

What would happen if we adopted that same attitude? What if we were willing to do whatever He told us? I want to have this type of heart toward Jesus. Can you imagine what the servants thought when He told them to fill all six jars with water? They must have thought He was crazy.

Are you willing to do whatever Jesus tells you, even if it seems ridiculous? I once heard a story about a woman in South Korea who the Lord told to do cartwheels across the stage of the church during a Sunday morning service. She went to her pastor and shared what she felt was from the Lord.

If a woman came up to me on a Sunday and wanted to do cartwheels across our stage, I highly doubt I would go with it. But this pastor knew her well and trusted that what she heard was from the Lord. Because of that, he allowed it. He introduced her and said they were going to do something unusual, but they felt they were being led by the Holy Spirit.

Across the stage she went doing cartwheels. I bet most people thought they were crazy. As she came to the end, a man sitting in the balcony cried out to God. He ran to the altar and surrendered his life to the Lord. Astonishingly, he had dared God on his way to church that day that, if He was real and was who He said He was, He should cause someone to do cartwheels in the church. God used that woman's faith and obedience, as well as the faith and obedience of the church leadership, to answer that skeptic's doubt.

The Lord spoke powerfully to me one evening before I became a pastor. I used to work for a jewelry store. After I got off work one Friday evening, I had to go to a department store in the next city over from where I live. I was tired and just wanted to go home as soon as I could.

Walking out of the mall, I felt the Lord say, "Go back to the end of the mall." I quickly dismissed it because I felt exhausted. But the Lord spoke again to my heart. I knew God wanted me to go back, but I didn't know why. Suddenly the thought came to me that perhaps God was going to have me run into a local pastor and he would have me speak at his church. Before I became a pastor, I spoke in all kinds of churches nearly every weekend.

I got my second wind, and began to walk through the large mall. I was looking intently at everyone, wondering when I would come across a pastor. Looking back, I bet people thought I was crazy because I looked so closely for someone I knew. When I came to the end of the mall, my heart sunk. I had felt so certain that I had heard the Lord say to go back. I felt silly, embarrassed, and even more exhausted.

I was about twenty feet from the end of the mall, staring at a large gray wall. I felt the Lord say, "You are not done. Go all the way to the end." I felt even sillier, more embarrassed, and, yes, even more exhausted. But my heart has always been sensitive to the Lord. So I walked another twenty feet in obedience to what I felt the Lord had told me. When I reached the end of the wall, I literally touched my nose to it. I felt the Lord say clearly to my heart, "You obeyed what I said! If you will love Me every day of your life the way you looked for a pastor in this mall, you will find Me every single day. Seek Me. Search for Me and you will find Me."

Now, it may not seem like very much to you, but that was a life-altering moment for me. What felt like a small, trivial, insignificant thing to me was important to the Lord. He wanted my full obedience. I have no doubt this one experience opened many more blessings in my life.

Because God could trust me with such a small detail, it would not be long until God would call me to plant Preaching Christ Church. I was so scared and told the Lord that no family would attend the church of a twenty-year-old who wasn't married and didn't have kids. Yet God knew what He was doing, and God knew I would obey Him. I might have doubts, fears, perhaps even arguments, but at the end of the day, I obey what He tells me to do.

Do you have that type of obedience? Can God depend on you attempting what He calls you to do, even if it is as silly as filling six stone pots with water when in reality you need wine?

The point is, what is your need? Have you invited Jesus into your need? Are you willing to do exactly what He tells you? If so, you will find your life blessed, and God will have the ability to move mountains for you.

God does not measure our lives by skills, talents, or any other abilities. God measures us by faith and obedience. If you are the least among your family or even the least talented among your church, God can still use you in remarkable ways. Stepping out in faith and obedience is something any Christ follower can do. The question is, will you?

"And he told them a parable to the effect that they ought always to pray and not lose heart. He said, 'In a certain city there was a judge who neither feared God nor respected man. And there was a widow in that city who kept coming to him and saying, "Give me justice against my adversary." For a while he refused, but afterward he said to himself, "Though I neither fear God nor respect man, yet because this widow keeps bothering me, I will give her justice, so that she will not beat me down by her continual coming." And the Lord said, 'Hear what the unrighteous judge says. And will not God give justice to his elect, who cry to him day and night? Will he delay long over them? I tell you, he will give justice to them speedily. Nevertheless, when the Son of Man comes, will he find faith on earth?'" (Luke 18:1-8)

Chapter Nine
Persistent Prayer

"...to the effect that they ought always to pray and not lose heart."
Luke 18:1

You may be in a difficult season where praying and trusting in the Lord is becoming more difficult. For this chapter, my aim is to show you what to do when God seems silent. Paul tells us that there are times we must push through in prayer. He says, "Be joyful in hope, patient in afflictions, faithful in prayer" (Romans 12:12 (NIV)).

Have there been times that you have needed to be faithful in prayer? I think to be faithful in prayer means that you keep on praying even when you feel like giving up. It means you have that much confidence in prayer and confidence in the faithfulness of God that you keep praying. The Parable of the Persistent Widow is a great gift to those who are discouraged and ready to give up on prayer. Ponder what Paul means by remaining faithful in prayer.

Persevering in prayer is one of the most difficult journeys in a believer's life, but it can also be one of the most rewarding. Together, we are going to study the Parable of the Persistent Widow found in Luke 18. I know you will find this story encouraging. It is my hope that it deepens your confidence in a God who promises to help us and answer prayer.

We Ought Always to Pray

So what did Jesus mean when He says we should pray "always"? A command like this can feel intimidating. I have heard stories of people who can pray for hours. I have often doubted if I could pray for hours on end. I'm not sure I could do anything for hours on end, but yet, Jesus commands us to pray "always."

Paul reaffirms Jesus' command to always pray in 1 Thessalonians 5:17. It says, "Pray without ceasing." How does someone accomplish this when we work jobs, raise families and juggle the other responsibilities of life? Does this command mean that we are to always have audible, memorized prayers on our lips?

I don't think the Bible is instructing audible prayers. As a matter of fact, Jesus warned against canned, religious prayers. He called them "vain." Matthew 6:7 says, "And when you pray, do not heap up empty phrases as the Gentiles do, for they think they will be heard for their many words."

God does not measure our praying by the amount of words we use nor by the amount of time we spend in prayer. If this is the case, then how does God measure prayer? The Bible tells us it is measured by our hearts. Jesus said in Matthew 5:18, "This people honors me with their lips, but their heart is far from me." This tells me that it matters to the Lord how I pray and if I am praying out of duty or from delight.

Prayer is so important to the Lord that He bottles them. The Psalmist wrote, "You keep track of all my sorrows. You have collected all my tears in your bottle. You have recorded each one in your book" (Psalm 56:8 (NLT)). If my prayers are that important then I should be aware of times I pray silly, self-centered prayers.

It matters to the Lord how we approach Him. Joel 2:12-13 teaches us how to seek the Lord. "'Yet even now,' declares the LORD, 'return to me with all your heart, with fasting, with weeping, and with mourning; and rend your hearts and not your garments.' Return to the LORD your God, for he is gracious and merciful, slow to anger, and abounding in steadfast love; and he relents over disaster."

If I am going to seek the Lord and pray "always," then I am going to keep my heart in tune and keep my spirit in a constant state of prayer, always ready to communicate with the Lord.

Do Not Lose Heart

No wonder Jesus says, "Do not lose heart." Prayer is a matter of the heart. So, if I am praying from my heart and keeping my spirit in a constant place of communicating with the Lord, it is going to be much easier to not grow discouraged when the going gets tough and prayer feels difficult.

Failure comes to prayer when we grow weary and quit. Have you ever felt like giving up on praying? I'm sure you've experienced a situation like this where you pray and your situation only grows worse. Often, the first thought we have is, "I should probably stop praying because it is making things worse." That is the exact strategy Satan has for our lives. For if he can hinder our praying, he can block the power of God that comes through prayer.

This is why Galatians 6:9 is so relevant to fighting discouragement. "And let us not grow weary of doing good, for in due season we will reap, if we do not give up." What a great verse to memorize when you are in a season of persevering prayer.

The Purpose of the Parable

Parables were among Christ's most favorite and creative ways to communicate the gospel. A parable is an earthly story with a heavenly meaning. Warren Wiersbe helps us understand the meaning of parables in his book *Meet Yourself in the Parables*. He says, "Parables are both mirrors and windows. As mirrors they help you see yourself. As windows they help you see life and God."

While the Bible records forty-six of Jesus' parables, it is important to note that not every detail of a parable is to be interpreted. Parables have one cardinal truth to share. The Bible is very clear about the purpose of this story. It is so we see the value of prayer and not lose heart and give up on calling on the name of the Lord.

The Judge

There are two characters Jesus introduces in this important story. We first meet the unjust judge. The office of a judge was an important role in Bible days. A judge was to be God's representative. 2 Chronicles 19:6-7 says, "...Consider what you do, for you judge not for man but for the LORD, He is with you in giving judgment. Now then, let the fear of the LORD be upon you. Be careful what you do, for there is no injustice with the LORD your God, or partiality or taking bribes."

It is important to understand that the unjust judge does not represent God. Jesus is contrasting God's faithfulness to the actions of the unjust judge. So it is not a representation, it is a sharp contrast.

The Bible says of this man that he neither feared God nor respected man. There is an important lesson here. If people who are in authority do not fear the Lord, then they naturally will not respect the laws of man. The two go together. This judge did not care about the needs of the widow because he had no regard for the Lord.

The Widow

In the Parable of Luke 18, it seems someone has taken advantage of this widow. The law seems to be on her side because she consistently pursues justice.

God has a great deal to say about the treatment of widows in the Bible. He cares deeply because widows were often defenseless and could easily be taken advantage of. James 1:27 says, "Religion that is pure and undefiled before God the Father is this: to visit orphans and widows in their affliction, and to keep oneself unstained from the world." This is how important the treatment of widows is to the Lord. We can see why Jesus uses this as an example.

For further study on God's expectations of the treatment of widows, read Exodus 22:22-24; Deuteronomy 10:18, 24:17, 27:19; Job 22:9, 24:3; Psalm 146:9; Isaiah 1:17,23; Jeremiah 7:6-7, 22:3; and Ezekiel 22:7.

His Refusal and Her Persistence

In Luke 18:3 it says the widow, "...kept coming to him and saying, 'Give me justice against my adversary.' For a while he refused..." This widow was quite persistent. Even though the judge refused her many requests, eventually he gives in. Luke 18:4-5 says, "...yet because this widow keeps bothering me, I will give her justice, so that she will not beat me down by her continual coming."

The word *beat* in verse 5 literally means "to black an eye." The imagery is that of a boxer being stunned and bruised. It could also be translated as "strike." Isn't that an incredible picture of persistence?

Once again, Jesus is not comparing God to the unrighteous judge. Instead, Jesus is teaching us that if an unrighteous judge can give justice, how much more is God, who is the Righteous Judge, willing to grant justice to His people?

Now Jesus is going to bring application to the parable. Notice verse 6 says, "And the Lord said." It is as if Luke is saying, "Now pay close attention because this is the main point."

Justice Given to the Elect

Why did Jesus use the word *elect* when He said, "And will not God give justice to his elect"? Why not use the term "my people" or "God's people?" The word *elect* can be a controversial term in many circles. Is there a connection between the word *elect* and the purpose of the parable? I think there is.

I struggled with the doctrine of election for quite some time. It became clearer for me when I was invited to speak at an evangelism conference in Cairo, Egypt, in 2007. For one of the sessions, the text the Lord kept placing on my heart was from the Old Testament, and it did not say flattering things about the Egyptian people. As a matter of fact, it showed God's hatred toward the Egyptians.

I kept thinking and praying, "Lord, I cannot read this aloud in an Egyptian church. Surely people will be offended, and I'll never be asked back to this event again." But the more I prayed (and squirmed), the more God pressed it upon my heart. Finally, I went to the conference pastor, who is also Egyptian. I asked him, "Pastor, how do you preach such difficult texts to your people? Is it not offensive to them?"

To my surprise, he smiled and said, "Chad, we believe in divine election. We understand that, just as we are God's elect today, Israel was also God's elect, chosen people." The Lord used this incident to open my eyes to divine election. I preached the text, and God blessed our service with His presence.

Over time, I began to see the beautiful doctrine of election for myself. Jesus makes it very clear that we did not choose Him. Rather,

He chose us. Think over John 15:16: "You did not choose me, but I chose you and appointed you that you should go and bear fruit and that your fruit should abide, so that whatever you ask the Father in my name, he may give it to you." Did you notice how Jesus links election with praying? Because He has chosen us, we can now ask Him for what we need and the Father will help us!

What is difficult to understand about election is that the Bible teaches both God's part in salvation as well as man's part. Just as God draws us to salvation, man has a responsibility to repent of sin and turn to the Lord. It can be difficult to reconcile the two. What I find fascinating is that the Bible does not seem to feel the need to defend man's responsibility over God's responsibility. It teaches both! I see it as a two-sided coin. Both are vital to salvation.

So again, back to my question, why does Jesus use the word *elect*? I believe it is because it magnifies the great love God the Father has for us. For me, it is a great reminder that when I pray, I am praying as God's elect. I am approaching God because He chose me and saved me by His grace.

Read Ephesians 1:4-5 carefully, "Even as he chose us in him before the foundation of the world, that we should be holy and blameless before him. In love, he predestined us for adoption to himself as sons through Jesus Christ, according to the purpose of his will." For me, those are beautiful phrases in the Bible. "To the purpose of his will" shows me that my salvation was not because of my decision to follow Jesus. Rather, it is because God came to me, a dead sinner, placed His love and grace over my life, and awakened my dead heart to the gospel.

When you realize Ephesians 1:5 teaches that our salvation is due to the will and purposes of God, then you can see more clearly what Jesus meant in John 1:13 when he spoke of the new birth: "Who were born, not of blood, nor of the will of the flesh, nor of the will of man, but of God."

Add to that 2 Timothy 1:9: "Who saved us and called us to a holy calling, not because of our works but because of his own purpose and grace, which he gave us in Christ Jesus before the ages began." And lastly, Titus 3:5, which says, "He saved us, not because of works done by us in righteousness, but according to his own mercy, by the washing of regeneration and renewal of the Holy Spirit."

All of these Scriptures make it evident that God has set His love upon us and saved us because it was His desire, not our own. How do you view your salvation? Do you see it as something you accomplished because you prayed a certain prayer or did a certain work? Or do you see salvation as a gift from God (Ephesians 2:8) and a work of grace initiated and completed by Jesus (Hebrews 12:2)?

This is an important and Biblical perspective to have because it speaks volumes to the way we pray. If I can understand divine election, then it greatly changes the way in which I approach God. I am not coming to Him begging for His attention or pleading for Him to see my needs. Instead, I am approaching my Heavenly Father who "Predestined us to adoption to Himself..." (Ephesians 1:5).

This means when I pray, I'm not throwing up "Hail Mary's" or "I hope God hears me" types of prayers. No! I am confident in Who my Father is. I am aware of His love and providence in my life. I am not approaching God from my own merits or from my own works, but instead from His grace. I believe this is why Jesus uses the word *elect*.

For further study on election, read these Scriptures: John 6:44; Romans 8:20-30; Romans 9:16; Acts 13:48; Acts 16:14; Ephesians 1:4-5, 11; Ephesians 2:8; 2 Thessalonians 2:13; 2 Timothy 1:9; 1 Peter 1:2; and 1 Peter 1:20

Who Cry to Him Day and Night

When I think of someone praying day and night, I think of David's transparent prayer, "I am worn out from my groaning. All night I flood my bed with weeping and drench my couch with tears" (Psalm 6:6 (NIV)).

Have you experienced burdens so heavy that it consumed your thoughts both day and night? While we may bring our cares before the Lord both day and night, this is not suggesting that we pray out of fear nor lack of faith. Actually, Christ challenges the lack of faith in prayer in the final verse of the section by asking in verse 8, "...When the Son of Man comes, will He find faith on the earth?"

We must be careful to always approach the Lord in faith, whether we are carrying burdens or not. Hebrews 11:6 says, "And without faith it is impossible to please him, for whoever would draw near to God must believe that he exists and that he rewards those who seek him." Examine the way you typically pray. Is it rooted in faith, knowing that God is both able and willing, or is it more like rolling the dice, hoping that God is going to hear you and acknowledge your need? According to Hebrews 11:6, faith is a requirement to pleasing the Lord...especially in prayer.

Persistent prayer that believes deeply in God's ability to answer is powerful and effective. We understand that any time spent before the Lord is not wasted time. We must believe that God is faithful and that He will respond. The next phrase of the text deepens our confidence even more.

Speedily

Jesus reminds us in verse 8 that God will not delay and that He will act on our behalf, "speedily." Why would Jesus need to tell us this? One commentator notes that time passes at different speeds with various seasons of life.

For example, my girls are five and three years old. Everyone constantly tells me that they will be grown in a blink of an eye, and I believe them. Whereas when we face a fierce trial, it can seem like time stands still. The temptation to give in to discouragement and give up are much greater in times of testing. Jesus knows this and so He reminds us that even though it doesn't feel like it, He is working on our behalf and He is working, "Speedily."

What a great reminder from God's Word the next time you are about to give up and stop praying! It is not God's faithfulness that is in question, it is our persevering that is in jeopardy. So be encouraged in your situation. Deliverance is closer than you think! When you pray, remind the Lord that you know, based on Luke 18, that He is working speedily on your behalf and thank Him for what you know He is doing. That my friends, is praying in faith!

Avoid the temptation to take matters into your own hands. Trust in the Lord and consider these promises from the Bible. "Entrusting himself to Him who judges justly" (1 Peter 2:23). "Beloved, never avenge yourselves, but leave it to the wrath of God, for it is written, 'Vengeance is mine, I will repay, says the Lord'" (Romans 12:19). "For His judgements are true and just" (Revelation 19:2).

An Odd Question

Jesus finished this parable with what seems to be an odd question. He asks, "Nevertheless, when the Son of Man comes, will He find faith on the earth?" What do you suppose He means by this?

Paul teaches that the last days will be dangerous times that try our faith. He outlines what the last days will look like in 2 Timothy 3. I think Jesus is asking His readers if there will still be people who are crying out to the Lord by the time the last days arrive.

For me this is a challenging and thought-provoking statement by Jesus. It says that when He returns, it is faith that He is looking for. People who are praying and crying out for righteous justice. Will He find it?

Once again, the theme is not that God is unfaithful but actually the opposite. If the wicked, unjust judge will grant justice, how much more so will a loving, gracious, righteous Father give justice to those who love Him and to those who are His elect?

Knowing that God is faithful to His Word should produce faithfulness in us, His people. However, Jesus understands how trying the times will be. Therefore, He reminds the Church that as we are patiently awaiting His return, know that He is coming to look for people of faith who are crying out to the Lord.

The Parable of the Persistent Widow should cause us to pause and pray for the coming of Christ. Note how John the Beloved prayed in Revelation 22:20, "...Even so, come quickly, Lord." This should be our prayer as well.

Did you know that Christ is coming with rewards ready for those who have been faithfully looking for His return? "Behold, I am coming soon, bringing my recompense with me, to repay each one for what he has done" (Revelation 22:12).

Lastly, the Bible teaches us that there is a crown prepared for those who love the appearing of the Lord. Let's look at 2 Timothy 4:8: "Henceforth there is laid up for me a crown of righteousness, which the Lord, the righteous judge, will award to me on that Day, and not only to me but also to all who have loved his appearing."

Did you see the name Paul used to describe the Lord? He calls Him the Righteous Judge! How fitting when we contrast the faithfulness of the Lord and the refusal of the unjust judge of Luke 18. Yes, my friends, the Lord is the Righteous Judge and He will faithfully execute justice on our behalf. Surely, the Lord will fight for us and show Himself strong in our lives. Keep serving and keep trusting until the day Jesus Christ returns.

"And they came to Jericho. And as he was leaving Jericho with his disciples and a great crowd, Bartimaeus, a blind beggar, the son of Timaeus, was sitting by the roadside. And when he heard that it was Jesus of Nazareth, he began to cry out and say, 'Jesus, Son of David, have mercy on me!' And many rebuked him, telling him to be silent. But he cried out all the more, 'Son of David, have mercy on me!' And Jesus stopped and said, 'Call him.' And they called the blind man, saying to him, 'Take heart. Get up; he is calling you.' And throwing off his cloak, he sprang up and came to Jesus. And Jesus said to him, 'What do you want me to do for you?' And the blind man said to him, 'Rabbi, let me recover my sight.' And Jesus said to him, 'Go your way; your faith has made you well.' And immediately he recovered his sight and followed him on the way." (Mark 10:46-52)

Chapter Ten
Crying Out All the More

"And many rebuked him, telling him to be silent. But he cried out all the more, 'Son of David, have mercy on me.'" Mark 10:48

One of the best ways to study the Bible is verse by verse and line upon line. When people ask me how I read the Bible, I always say, "Very slowly." I would rather read one verse and have the Lord speak to me than to read an entire book of the Bible as fast as I can. When we read God's Word slowly and give room for the Holy Spirit to speak to us, the Bible opens up in a new and fresh way.

It was Charles Spurgeon who said, "No one outgrows Scripture. The Book widens and deepens with our years." I have found this true throughout my years of preaching the Bible. It does not matter how many times I have preached from a certain passage, it seems the Bible is always fresh, relevant, and ready to bear new fruit in my life. Such is the case with Blind Bartimaeus. Many of you may have grown up learning about his story. It is my prayer God will have new things to say to you from his incredible encounter with Christ.

Jesus and Jericho

It must have been something special to walk through Jericho with Jesus. It was not an ordinary city and Jesus was not an ordinary Rabbi. Of course we know Jericho from the Old Testament and the supernatural victory God gave to Joshua and Israel recorded in Joshua 6. But it was also a very important city in Jesus' day. The Jewish historian Josephus tells us a great deal about Jericho.

Jesus was passing through Jericho on his way to Jerusalem because the time had come for him to die on the cross. It was Passover and Jericho was only fifteen miles from Jerusalem. Can you imagine all that was on Jesus' mind? He knew he was about to be betrayed and delivered over to death. He was about to give His life as the Lamb of God and be sacrificed for our sins. The "bitter cup" was coming quickly.

Even though Jesus had the pressure of His imminent and violent death on his mind, He still had time to stop and minister to others. John MacArthur, a renowned Bible scholar, likens Zacchaeus and Bartimaeus as his final two trophies of saving, sovereign grace until the cross.

A Blind Beggar Named Bartimaeus

I have chosen Mark's account for this chapter because it is believed that Mark was an eyewitness to this miracle. The detail with which he writes is captivating. He names Bartimaeus specifically as the son of Timaeus. It might seem like a discrepancy when you read the other Gospels, because Mark only mentions Bartimaeus while Matthew and Luke mention two beggars. Why would Mark omit the other beggar?

I agree with Bible commentators who say that silence is not contradiction. Just because Mark does not mention Bartimaeus' companion does not mean the narrative is wrong.

Many believe it is because Bartimaeus went on to follow Jesus, as the end of Mark 10 suggests, and that he became a prominent and well-known figure in the early church. So when Mark wrote his gospel account, people would be able to identify Bartimaeus because he was still following the Lord.

We are not told why Bartimaeus was blind, how long he had been blind, or what had caused his condition. Was he born this way, as was the blind man in John 9? Was it caused by poor sanitary conditions or could it have been by an unfortunate accident? The Bible does not tell us. What we do know is that he was poor, because in those days, there was not any type of government safety net, like disability. The only way Bartimaeus could survive was to be dependent on the generosity of strangers. So he sat alongside the road asking for charity.

Great Crowds Were on the Road

There were two reasons why the crowds swelled in Jericho in Mark 10. First, as mentioned earlier, it was Passover. The city would have been buzzing as countless people were making their way to Jerusalem, which was only a six-hour walk from Jericho.

Second, word was spreading about Jesus. It had spread to the extent that even Blind Bartimaeus had heard about His miracles. Bethany was a nearby community and everyone had heard how Lazarus had been dead for three days until Jesus arrived and raised him from the dead. If the *Jerusalem Post* had been around back then, Jesus would have made the front page...a lot!

Jesus, Son of David, Have Mercy on Me

While most people called Him Jesus of Nazareth, it was the blind beggar who had the best spiritual 20/20 vision. He cried out to Jesus in a most unusual way, saying, "Jesus, Son of David, have mercy on me." Those must have been sweet words in the ears of Jesus because Bartimaeus recognized that Jesus was not just a Nazarene. It would not be long before the crowds would trade Barabbas, a murderer, for Jesus. The Roman Soldiers would pluck His beard, rip and gamble for His clothing, crown Him with thorns, and put a sign above His cross, mocking Him as the "King of the Jews." This blind beggar saw Jesus for who He really is, the Son of God!

Many Rebuked Him, Telling Him to Be Silent

You can imagine the scene as Jesus drew closer, and more and more people lined the streets. If you were a blind beggar, where would the best place be to set up for business? It would have probably been in the streets, asking for alms as people made their way to the Passover.

But this day was different for Bartimaeus. He wasn't asking for alms. He was asking to see Jesus. Why were the crowds so rude to him? Wouldn't someone out of compassion help him to get a front-row seat in hopes that Jesus may touch and heal him? Why would they rebuke him as Mark 10:48 describes?

I believe it was because, in their culture, they viewed blindness as a curse from God. Remember when the disciples asked Jesus what caused the man in John 9 to be blind? Was it his parents' sin or his own sin? Jesus corrected their thinking in John 9:3 by saying, "It was not that this man sinned, or his parents, but that the works of God might be displayed in him."

There is a great spiritual application here for the Church. Should we not be seeking those who are spiritually blind and bringing them to Jesus? Paul teaches us that those who are without Christ are "blinded." 2 Corinthians 4:4 states, "In their case the god of this world has blinded the minds of unbelievers, to keep them from seeing the light of the gospel of the glory of Christ, who is the image of God." Those who are lost are spiritually blind, and we should be guiding them to Christ. On this day, the crowd rebuked him and tried to quiet him, whereas they should have been helping and guiding him to the Healer.

He Cried Out All the More

Bartimaeus would not be quieted! Mark 10:48 tells us that when the crowd rebuked him and tried to quiet him, Bartimaeus cried out all the more. I love that phrase! This is what true, desperate praying looks like.

Have you ever cried out to Jesus? I mean the type of crying out that happens when you know Jesus is the only One who can help you, when everyone else has tried and failed. There is a type of desperation God responds to. Psalm 18:6 teaches us about this type of desperate prayer: "In my distress I called upon the LORD; to my God I cried for help. From his temple he heard my voice, and my cry to him reached his ears." How comforting it is that the Lord hears us.

Bartimaeus cried out all the more because he refused to allow anyone to hinder him getting to Jesus. I want this type of resolve in my prayer life. If I know God can help me, then I am not going to let anyone stop me from getting to God!

And Jesus Stopped

Mark 10:49 is one of the sweetest verses in the Gospels. It says, "And Jesus stopped and called him..." Now remember what is happening. Jesus is on His way to Calvary. His death is imminent and much is weighing on His mind. He knows he will face Judas Iscariot and Pontius Pilate and will hang between two thieves. Even though He knows all of these events are about to transpire, He stops to help a blind beggar.

He had just taught His disciples about servanthood in Mark 10:43-45. This is right before the account of Blind Bartimaeus. He said, "But whoever would want to be great among you must be your servant, and whoever would be first among you must be slave to all. For even the Son of Man came not to be served but to serve and to give his life a ransom for many."

What a beautiful Savior! The King had become the servant. He was on the road to the cross, yet He made time for a poor blind beggar. Do you believe you have the attention of the Savior when you pray?

Robert Murray M'Cheyne, a Scottish pastor of the 1800s said, "If I could hear Christ praying for me in the next room, I would not fear a million enemies. Yet distance makes no difference. He is praying for me."

Oh to be near Christ! To enjoy His fellowship and commune with Him. Yes, you can be near Him. You have His attention. Call on His name and see how close He is to you! Just as He gave Bartimaeus His attention, so He will kindly and graciously give us the same affection and the same attention.

Jesus Calls for Him

Throughout Jesus's earthly ministry, He was never impressed with crowds. They flocked to Him, but it always seemed He looked past them to the individual who needed Him most. This was the case with Blind Bartimaeus.

How many people wanted a moment with Him? How many had questions and wanted to hear Him teach? But who did Jesus call for? The one whom He heard the voice of faith from...Blind Bartimaeus!

Throwing Off His Cloak, He Sprang to His Feet

It is interesting that Bartimaeus did not hesitate once he learned he had the attention of Jesus. Notice what Mark writes in verse 50: "And throwing off his cloak, he sprang up and came to Jesus."

What was the cloak he wore? Perhaps it protected him from the weather. Maybe it was a gift from his past. Whatever the case, it represented his old life, and he quickly laid it aside to respond to Jesus.

There are many who are not willing to do this. They want Jesus, but they want their old "cloaks" too. They want to hang on to their old lifestyles. They want to keep what is familiar to them close by. We must realize, though, that following Jesus is radical. It demands change.

Bartimaeus' cloak represents his old lifestyle, and he was willing to lay it aside. Are you willing to do the same? Have you walked away from your past and shut the door on the temptation it offers? The author of Hebrews shows us how to go forward in our faith. He writes in Hebrews 12:1, "Therefore, since we are surrounded by so great a cloud of witnesses, let us also lay aside every weight, and sin which clings so closely, and let us run with endurance the race that is set before us, looking to Jesus, the founder and perfecter of our faith..." You will never run a race worthy of Christ while hanging on to your old lifestyle.

What Do You Want Me to Do for You?

Jesus asked him an interesting question when He posed, "What do you want me to do for you?" I'm curious as to why Jesus would ask a blind beggar what he wanted. Did Jesus not know he wanted his sight more than anything?

Andrew Murray, the author of the classic book *With Christ in the School of Prayer*, offers this suggestion. He says we are often vague with the Lord in our prayer requests. We ask the Lord to help us, but we do not take the time to talk to the Lord about specific areas of our life where we need His help. We ask the Lord to remove sin, but we do not pray against that sin by name. Quite often, we pray in an ambiguous way.

This question by Jesus, to a man who is obviously blind, should teach us how specific the Lord wants our requests to be. This encourages my heart when I realize how Christ wants me to tell Him everything that is in my heart!

It is also interesting to note that this is the second time in Mark 10 that Jesus asks, "What do you want me to do for you?" In verses 35-37, John and James approached Jesus to ask him for a favor. Jesus asked them what they wanted and their response was, "Grant us to sit, one at your right hand and one at your left, in your glory."

I wonder if Jesus let out a loud sigh. After three years of teaching, discipling, and modeling, here they were, a week away from Calvary, and they still didn't get it. His followers are arguing over who will be the greatest in the Kingdom. But not Blind Bartimaeus. When the King of kings and the Lord of lords asked him what he wanted from Him, Bartimaeus didn't hesitate.

Again, this is a great evangelistic lesson to the Church. Do you know what happens when fishermen do not fish? We fight! Christ has called us to fish for souls. Mark 1:17 says, "Follow me, and I will make you fishers of men." Jesus came to seek and to save the lost, not argue over who would be the greatest in the Kingdom.

We do the same in the Church today. We compare ourselves to other ministries and larger churches. We ask God to bless others, but we do not really mean it, not if it means God would bless their work more than our own. If you and I will focus on the Blind Bartimaeus of this world, there will be no room for our egos, pride, or arrogance. God will be glorified through changed lives and we will share in that joy.

Rabbi, Let Me Recover My Sight

The crowd gathered because they wanted to hear the Rabbi's teaching. Bartimaeus cried out because he needed Jesus! Is it not the same in our culture today? So many attend church but to what end? To only hear better sermons? We have more teaching available than at any other time in church history. Look how many books, sermon series, and other teaching formats are developed and published each year. But how many from within the Church are desperate and crying out for Jesus?

By calling him "Rabbi," he recognized Jesus as a distinguished teacher, but this blind beggar could see far better than most that Jesus was more than a good teacher. He was the Son of God.

Bartimaeus Hymn

John Newton, the author of the timeless hymn "Amazing Grace," also wrote a hymn about the blind beggar simply entitled "Bartimaeus."

"Mercy, O thou Son of David! Thus Blind Bartimaeus prayed; Others by thy word are saved, Now to me afford thine aid; Many for his crying chide him, But he called the louder still; Till the gracious Savior bid him, 'Come, and ask me what you will.' Money was not what he wanted, Though by begging used to live; But he asked, and JESUS granted alms, which none but he could give; LORD remove this grievous blindness, Let my eyes behold the day; Straight he saw, and won by kindness, Followed JESUS in the way; O! Methinks I hear him praising, Publishing to all around; 'Friends, is not my case amazing? What a Savior I have found; O! That all the blind but knew him, And would be advised by me! Surely, would they hasten to him? He would cause them all to see.'"

Go Your Way

Jesus says to him in Mark 10:52, "Go your way, your faith has made you well." I cannot imagine what those words meant to Bartimaeus. When others rebuked, sneered at, and scolded him, he cried out all the more, and now it had paid off.

What would it mean to a blind beggar for Jesus to say, "Go your way"? Think about that. For the first time he could work a job and earn an income, whereas before, he was dependent on people and their charity. For the first time, he could visit with friends and loved ones and see their faces and reactions. Life would no longer be lonely and burdensome. What would he do with such a life?

When Jesus told Bartimaeus to "go your way," He was telling him that his walk with Christ was dependent on faith. Faith in Jesus had made him well. You can go your own way independent of Christ. Does that describe your relationship with the Lord? If God brings you the miracle of salvation, will your faith carry you the rest of the walk? Luke 9:23 commands us, "If anyone would come after me, let him deny himself and take up his cross daily and follow me." Are you following Christ in this manner or have you gone "your way" rather than His way?

Followed Him on the Way

The last phrase of Mark 10:52 tells us, "...Immediately he recovered his sight and followed Him on the way." Isn't that remarkable? There wasn't anything about his old life that kept him in Jericho. Nothing compared to following Jesus. Mark makes it clear that he followed him out of Jericho.

What do you think the fifteen mile walk from Jericho to Jerusalem was like through the new eyes of Bartimaeus? I wonder if he experienced the triumphal entry. I wonder if he told everyone he met how Jesus had opened his eyes that week.

Could it be that Bartimaeus saw Jesus die on the cross? Could he have been one of the followers who saw Jesus ascend to heaven in Acts 1? Perhaps he was among the Christ followers who experienced the Holy Spirit in the Upper Room in Acts 2?

Many Bible commentators believe that Blind Bartimaeus was a well-known person in the early church, and they believe this is why Mark mentions him specifically by name. I would agree.

"Is anyone among you suffering? Let him pray. Is anyone cheerful? Let him sing praise. Is anyone among you sick? Let him call for the elders of the church, and let them pray over him, anointing him with oil in the name of the Lord. And the prayer of faith will save the one who is sick, and the Lord will raise him up. And if he has committed sins, he will be forgiven. Therefore, confess your sins to one another and pray for one another, that you may be healed. The prayer of a righteous person has great power as it is working. Elijah was a man with a nature like ours, and he prayed fervently that it might not rain, and for three years and six months it did not rain on the earth. Then he prayed again, and heaven gave rain, and the earth bore its fruit. My brothers, if anyone among you wanders from the truth and someone brings him back, let him know that whoever brings back a sinner from his wandering will save his soul from death and will cover a multitude of sins." (James 5:13-20)

Chapter Eleven

INTERCESSION: Getting in the Devil's Way

"O Lord, according to all your righteous acts, let your anger and your wrath turn away from your city Jerusalem, your holy hill, because for our sins, and for the iniquities of our fathers, Jerusalem and your people have become a byword among all who are around us." Daniel 9:19

Is there a prodigal in your life whose safety and salvation you often pray for? In this chapter we are going to explore how to pray skillful and effective prayers of intercession for the people we love. Our example for this chapter is going to be the prophet Daniel. The book of Daniel may be one of the most fascinating books of the entire Bible. It is packed full of remarkable stories of God supernaturally delivering his people. We are introduced to such blockbuster characters like the madman King Nebuchadnezzar and his golden statue, like the drunken King Belshazzar and the handwriting of God on the wall that brought his condemnation. We are also met with the defiant three Hebrew children—Shadrach, Meshach, and Abendigo—who defied the king's orders. They would not bow, they would not bend, and when they faced the king's fiery furnace, they were delivered by the hand of the Lord. Then of course we meet Daniel himself, who would not obey the king's orders to stop praying and faced a den of hungry lions for his capital punishment. As you know the story, God shut the mouths of those hungry lions, and Daniel used them as a pillow as he rested in the sovereign hand of God. Yes, Daniel is a remarkable book. But what I appreciate most out of these Scriptures is the richness of his prayer life. We are going to see for ourselves how Daniel was a model when it came to intercessory prayer.

When studying the way Daniel prayed, you and I can learn many life-changing principles to strengthen our own times of praying. Just as Jesus modeled how to approach the Father and how to pray effectively in Matthew chapter 6, so Daniel is going to model for us in chapter 9 how to approach the King of kings and the Lord of lords. Scholars tell us that at this point in Daniel's life he is approximately eighty years old. It is important to remember that the book of Daniel is not written in chronological order. Therefore, when we come to chapter 9. This is an older, wiser Daniel that is modeling prayer for us.

If you remember, Daniel was born in Judea but was taken captive and led away to the Babylonian Empire. He was taken as a slave to serve the kings of Babylon, and Daniel grew up around them, serving them. When reading Daniel 9, you should remember that he has had a lifetime of experience approaching and petitioning kings. He is now going to show us how to come before God Almighty, who is the King of kings and Lord of lords. Studying chapter 9, you and I are going to be able to come to the Royal Courts of God and plead our case before the Lord God Almighty.

The Meaning of Intercession

For many Christians, intercessory prayer can be intimidating. It feels as though this type of praying is reserved for the elite of believers. My friends, this is not the case. God invites us all to this type of special praying. You can grow in your ability to intercede for others. You can gain the skill that Daniel had in the way he petitioned the Lord.

The term intercession means to intervene on behalf of someone else. When you pray intercessory prayers, you are petitioning the Lord on behalf of other people. What a stark contrast that is from the way most Christians pray today. As we have already explored through the previous chapters of this book, much of our praying is self-centered. If God were to give us the ability to go back and listen to all of our prayers, how many of them would be focused only on our wants and needs.

Intercessory prayer is focuses on the needs of others. It is when we stand in the gap on behalf of those we love and petition God for their needs. My favorite definition of intercession is to get in the way of the devil. This is exactly what happens when we choose to engage in intercessory prayer. We put ourselves between Satan and the ones we love, and God uses us to frustrate and hinder the plots, schemes, and tactics of the enemy. A great Biblical example of intercessory prayer is when Abraham intercedes for his nephew Lot and his family in Sodom and Gomorrah. If you remember the story in Genesis 18, Lot was reluctant to leave the city. The angels came to warn Lot of the coming judgment of God, but he refused to leave the city he loved. After several failed attempts to convince Lot to leave the city, the angels took Lot by the arm and instructed him to leave immediately. In other words, they intervened. More importantly, they intervened because of Abraham's prayers. This is what happens when you pray for the people who you love the most. You are asking the Lord to take them by the arm and lead them out of harm's way. My friends, this is intercessory prayer. Satan would try to tell us that this type of praying can only be done by special types of Christians. No, this kind of praying is for you and me. These are the types of prayers that rescue people out of their sins and save them from destruction.

Another reason that intercessory prayer means so much to me is because this is the eternal ministry work of our Lord and Savior Jesus Christ. Hebrews 7:25 teaches that Christ ever lives to make intercession for us. That is a remarkable thought that, at this moment, Christ is praying for you. As you may remember from chapter 9, Robert Murray M'Cheyne made this incredible statement: "If I could hear Christ praying for me in the next room, I would not fear a million enemies. Yet distance makes no difference. He is praying for me." Do you feel as though Jesus Christ is interceding on your behalf? Do you feel as though he is working? When you and I come into the beautiful work of intercessory prayer, we are entering into the ministry that Christ is doing right now on our behalf. Now let us unpack Daniel 9 together and see the richness of Daniel's praying.

Self-Evaluation

Before I can effectively intercede on the behalf of others, I must first evaluate my own spiritual condition. Daniel 9:3 helps me in this self-evaluation. What strikes me about the way Daniel prayed is that his praying was not cold, mechanical, or routine. Rather, his praying was deliberate, intentional, and disciplined. I want you first to notice how he approached the Lord in verse three. He says, "Then I turned my face toward the Lord God." What I see in this phrase is that there is a deliberate turning to the Lord. When I read this phrase, it causes me to pause and ask if my prayer life is on autopilot. Am I simply going through the motions of prayer or am I seeking God by turning my face toward Him? If you are anything like me, it is easy to search for answers in other people. If I'm not careful, I seek answers in resources other than the Lord God. What Daniel teaches me in verse 9 is that, if I'm going to be serious about intercession, I must be serious about turning my attention toward the Lord and nothing else.

Second, I want you to notice the discipline Daniel has in his praying. Notice the spiritual elements Daniel has in his praying. He includes pleas for mercy, fasting, sackcloth and ashes. In other words, Daniel is seeking the Lord with pleas of mercy, fasting, humility and repentance. Are these elements of your spiritual prayer life? If you want to add dynamite to the way you pray, incorporate these elements. If you want to check to see if your prayer life has become routine, ask yourself these questions. When was the last time I called on the name of the Lord with pleas for mercy? When did I last pray the way Hannah prayed, not with her lips, but from her heart? When was the last time I sought the Lord with fasting included in my prayers? When was the last time I humbled myself under the mighty hand of God? Daniel did not approach the Lord with casual, aimless prayers. Do you?

I think one of the greatest tragedies is to live a haphazard Christian life. What do I mean by haphazard? I mean that many of us live careless and indifferent lives for the Lord. Many of us do not plan devotion times nor prayer times. Most of us do not plan our giving and tithing to the Lord. For so many, our Christian walk is a matter of convenience, not a matter of discipline. If your greatest desire is to know the Lord more, spiritual disciplines are one of the greatest paths to knowing God more intimately. Begin to incorporate discipline into your prayer life. Set times of fasting and times of humility, times of humbling yourself before the Lord, and you will naturally begin to set times of intercession for others. You will find yourself becoming more pleasing to the Lord, and He will be more of a delight to you.

A Personal God

As we come to verse four, I want to show you the foundation of why we can bring our personal pleas before God. If you pay attention in chapter 9, Daniel uses two different names for the Lord. You will notice that the word Lord in some cases is spelled with a capital L and the rest are lowercase. In other cases, the word Lord is in all capital letters. What is the difference? The title Lord with the L and lowercase letters is the Hebrew title for God, Adonai. It literally means Lord and Master. When we pray to Adonai, we recognize that God is the master of all things in our lives. Yet Daniel uses a different name for the Lord in verse four. It is God's personal name, Yahweh. Whenever you see the word Lord in all capital letters in the Old Testament, it is referencing God's personal name, which He revealed to Moses at the burning bush. I believe what this is saying to us is that we can bring the most personal needs of our life to God by calling on His personal name. We can bring the most intimate of requests. We can bring the people who we love the most and plea for mercy on their behalf because God is an incredibly personal God. He is not just Master. He is our Heavenly Father who takes interest and cares for us. If at times your prayer life seems distant, or perhaps it seems as though God is distant, take heart. Daniel teaches us to approach God. You can come to Him with all matters because God comes to us in a personal way by revealing His name and His character.

One of my favorite sermon series from my time preaching at Preaching Christ Church was a collection of sermons on the Hebrew names of God. We explored many of the rich names for God. The purpose of God revealing His name is so that we might understand His character. Daniel is going to pray toward the character of God. Note in Daniel 9:9 that he reminds the Lord that mercy and forgiveness belongs to Him. Because Daniel knew the character of God, he could pray toward the character of God. All of this has to do with his personal name, Yahweh. So, how do we find ourselves praying? Instead of praying out of our own goodness, merits, and self-righteousness, we begin to pray toward God's goodness, His promises, and ultimately His righteousness. Can you see how this shifts the focus of prayer away from us and places our focus on the Lord?

The Right Pattern of Praying.

Beginning with the end of verses 4-19, we see the right pattern for intercessory prayer. Daniel is going to teach us that when approaching a King, we begin with worship, continue by confessing our sin, and then make our request in prayer. Often we get the cart before the horse, reversing this important order. We begin our praying with the request, skipping the reverent worship and confession of sin. This is a very clear structure and an important principle to follow in our own praying.

Notice in verse 4 that Daniel reminds God that He is a God who keeps covenant with his people. Rather than Daniel coming to God with his concerns, he first comes with reverent worship. This is a step that Christians today miss all too often because we live in such a fast-paced culture. Frequently when we pray, we do not take the time to worship God the way we should. Think how different your prayer life would be if you spent more time worshiping the Lord rather than asking for what you have need of. Daniel worships the Lord and reminds God of His covenant and steadfast love for His people.

Do you feel it's wrong to remind God of His promises? I think this is a Biblical concept. If our attitude is humble and full of grace, it is a good thing to remind God of His great and precious promises. It says to the Lord that we literally take Him at His word, and I believe this glorifies God.

Daniel says to the Lord in verse four that he is a covenant-keeping God full of steadfast love. The word *love* here in the Hebrew is Hesed, which means loving-kindness. It speaks to the consistent love that God has for His people. God says I have loved you with an everlasting love (Jeremiah 31:3). Charles Stanley says it well: "There is nothing you can do to make God love you more and there's nothing you can do to make God love you less." God's love for us is consistent and unchanging.

Worship

Why do you suppose God would want us to begin our prayer times with worship rather than our needs? It causes us to put our focus and our attention in the right place. Imagine the fear and frustrations that would be removed from your heart if you focused more on God. Focus more on His greatness and His consistency, rather than on your ever-changing needs and emotions. It puts God in the right perspective and you see His greatness more than you see your problems.

Unfortunately, in our current church culture, we tend to view worship and prayer time as two separate elements. In reality, worship and prayer go together. As you include more worship in your praying, you will find that you pray with more humility. You will have a different experience with the Lord. As you seek to grow in your prayer life, start to add worship at the beginning of your prayer times. Humbly remind God of His word.

Confession

As we work our way to verse five, notice the transition in Daniel's prayer. He begins with worship and then moves into confession. This is such an important element in intercessory prayer. Christians must be careful that we are not spiritually aloof. We must be willing to confess our sins as well as the sins of the people we love. Confession of sin is such an important part of a strong prayer life and yet, in our culture, this is a missing piece of prayer. Confession simply means to agree with God. When we are willing to confess sin, it means that we are agreeing with God and what He calls sin. There are swift and dangerous currents moving through our culture today. Many of the problems we are seeing would diminish if the Church were willing to call sin what it is. If we are going to see God move in our country and see things turn around, Christians must lead the way in repentance and confession of sin. We must not point our fingers but instead fold our hands, repent, and confess sins. If the nation's repentance is going to come, it must come first from the Church of Jesus.

What I appreciate about Daniel's prayer is that the righteous prophet does not point out the sins of everyone else. Instead, he identifies with the sins of his people. If you pay close attention, you will notice that between verse 5 and 18, Daniel uses personal pronouns about thirty times. If we are to pray great prayers of intercession as Daniel models, we must identify with the sins of our country. May God grant us the right attitude and not say it is their sin, but rather say it is our sin. May we not say it is their problem, but may we say it is our problem. This is the beauty of intercession and pleas for mercy. How can we do this if we are spiritually arrogant? How can we make intercession on behalf of those who are sinning if we do not have grace and humility? The Church today should take note of the wise prophet Daniel and identify ourselves with the sins of our country as we plead for God to heal our land.

Request

At the time of this revision, Sadie and I are in an exciting and challenging time in parenting. Our girls, Piper and Emmy, are nine and seven years old. Our boys, Hudson and John Mark, are three and almost two. One thing is for certain about our children, they never hesitate to let us know what they want. Do you sometimes feel like you are a nuisance to God? Do you feel like you are bothering him constantly, reminding Him of your needs and His promises? Do not forget that the Bible encourages us to call on God. Our Heavenly Father tells us to call him our Abba or Poppa. Just as a good parent desires to know the wants and needs of their children, God desires to know what is going on in your life, and He wants you to bring your request to Him.

Now that Daniel has modeled for us how to worship the Lord and how to confess our sins, he is going to show us how to petition the King. Notice in verse 18 Daniel asked the Lord to incline His ear and hear his request, to open His eyes and see the needs. Notice what

Daniel did not do. He did not bring an attitude of arrogance nor entitlement. Daniel did not pray as though God owed him anything. Instead, he said it was not because of his righteousness that he brought this petition but because of God's great mercy. When you and I pray, could it be that there is a sense of entitlement? James 4:6 tells us the Lord gives greater grace to those who humble themselves. I hear a great deal of humility in Daniel as he approaches the King in verse 18. How would the response of God be different if we approached God, not out of our own righteousness, but because of God's great mercy?

Now Daniel is ready to petition the Lord. In verse 19 he says, "O Lord hear, O Lord forgive, O Lord pay attention, and act. Delay not for your own sake..." This is a perfect prayer. How many of us have prodigals we could speak this prayer over? Should you begin to incorporate this kind of praying into your request, I believe it would add explosive dynamite to your prayer life. Many well-meaning Christians pray to the Lord for their petitions but very few intercede. Our prayers would be much more effective if we followed Daniel's model of worship, confession, and bringing our request before the King. Our prayers would be more fruitful if we included the Word of God in our praying rather than our own thoughts, wants, and desires. Whoever the prodigal in your life is who is far from God, verses 18 and 19 would be the right way to pray for them. Do not skip worship and confession, and you will be able to effectively and skillfully bring the people you love before the royal court of heaven and find grace and help in your time of need from a loving King.

Chapter Twelve

Prayer That Avails

"...the prayer of a righteous person has great power as it is working."
James 5:16

The Bible teaches in James 5:16 that there is a type of praying that "avails." If there is a way to pray more effectively, then I want to learn how to pray in that way. At times, our prayers can become dull and stale. Have you had times when praying was mundane? James is going to teach us how to stay focused and how to pray with fervency.

As a pastor, I am aware that I am modeling prayer before my people. I try not to pray in an official or mechanical way. Everything I do models, as does everything I don't do. So if my people never hear me pray genuine, heartfelt prayers, what am I modeling? It communicates that spontaneous and authentic prayers are not important.

The same principle applies with my family. Do your children or grandchildren hear you pray? Can they see the love you have for the Lord in the way you talk to Him? If my wife and children do not hear me pray, then I have to ask myself if I am demonstrating the importance of spiritual growth and maturity.

As Christ followers, our most important responsibility is to pray. It was Oswald Chambers, author of the classic devotional *My Utmost for His Highest*, who wrote, "Prayer does not fit us for the greater work. Prayer is the greater work." When we can gain this type of perspective, prayer becomes the priority of our lives.

Like most, I face the temptation to get swept away in busyness. Each day, there is more to do than I can accomplish. Even though my life and work is ministry, I still have to make prayer my priority. Martin Luther, the great Protestant Reformer of the 1500s, was once asked what his plan for the coming day was. He responded, "Work, work, from early until late. In fact, I have so much to do that I shall spend the first three hours in prayer." Do we approach our days with this type of attitude? We all live under the pressure and busyness of life's responsibilities. How dependent are we on the help and strength of the Lord? Throughout the chapters of this book, we have learned how we should be giving our energy to praying and trusting in the Lord rather than living in our own strength. When we consider how much help the Lord wants to give us, why would we not be more persistent in prayer?

Confidence in Prayer

Why does God answer certain prayers while others seem to go unanswered? There are several answers to this question and, by studying James 5, the Bible will do what it is intended to do. Scripture says of itself in Psalm 119:105, "Your word is a lamp to my feet and a light to my path." Together, we will unpack what prevailing prayer looks like and how we can engage in it.

Jesus reminds us in Luke 18:1 that we should always pray and not give up (see chapter 8). Why would Jesus tell us not to give up in prayer? I think because He understands how discouraging unanswered prayer can be. If you are facing a season where you are frustrated and discouraged because of unanswered prayer, I want to encourage you to not give up because the Bible teaches us a way of praying that avails.

If You Are Suffering, Go Pray!

James, who is the author of the Epistle of James, was well acquainted with prayer. Hegesippus, a chronicler of the early church, tells us that James was nicknamed "Camel Knees" because of the frequency with which he prayed. So when James writes, under the inspiration of the Holy Spirit, and teaches us about prayer, we should especially take note of how this great man of prayer says prayer works.

Notice that James begins this section of chapter 5 by addressing the issue of suffering among believers. The Greek word James used for suffering is kakopathei. It means suffering of any kind. It could refer to sickness, which he will mention in the next verse. It could also mean bereavement, persecution, or even life's disappointments.

The answer is so simple, yet so neglected. When we face seasons of suffering, the Bible is clear in how we are to respond. It says we are to pray. I am thankful that James is going to give us specific details as to why and how we are to pray. He says it has great power as it is working, meaning it is radically effective. Is it not easy to forget the power of God when you are overwhelmed with life's circumstances or when you face hopeless situations?

At the heart of spiritual warfare is prayer. If Satan can discourage our desire to pray, then he knows he has the upper hand. This is why the Bible's teaching on prayer is so important to study and understand.

As I have faced times of discouragement, I have found the hymn "What A Friend We Have In Jesus" a great reminder to continue on in prayer.

"What a friend we have in Jesus, All our sins and griefs to bear! What a privilege to carry, Everything to God in prayer! Oh, what peace we often forfeit, Oh, what needless pain we bear, All because we do not carry, Everything to God in prayer!" If you are cheerful...sing!

There are two powerful Psalms that come to my mind when I think of singing to the Lord. The first is Psalm 59:16, "But I will sing of your strength; I will sing aloud of your steadfast love in the morning. For you have been to me a fortress and a refuge in the day of my distress."

Do you notice what David is saying? He is singing of the protection the Lord has given him. If you are in a place of weakness right now, do you realize how much it would help to sing of God's strength? If you focused more on His strength than your weakness, then you would experience what Paul meant in 2 Corinthians 12:9 when he said, "My grace is sufficient for you, for my power is made perfect in weakness. Therefore I will boast all the more gladly of my weaknesses, so that the power of Christ may rest upon me." Is that not fascinating that Paul says he can "boast all the more" in his weaknesses? What a different perspective in life! Paul concludes this verse by saying the result of this type of attitude is that, "The power of Christ may rest upon me." What is greater than Christ's power resting upon us in moments of weakness?

Another powerful Psalm in my life is Psalm 63:7. It says, "For you have been my help, and in the shadow of your wings I will sing for joy." Again, David is remembering how much the Lord has helped him. Can you think back to a time that God has been faithful to you? What special moments to sing over!

I can remember a time when the Lord was teaching me how to pray. I was very young, and it seemed I only prayed if I needed help or was in trouble. Very gently, the Lord told me that He wanted me to pray all the time. He explained how He wanted to know everything about my life—the good as well as the bad. As simple as it sounds, that is when I really began to talk with the Lord. Now I find myself talking to Him every day, all day!

Notice how James exhorts us. If anyone is cheerful, let him sing praises. Why does singing matter to the Lord? I believe it is because singing brings joy to our hearts and right perspective to our souls.

The Prayer of Faith Will Heal the Sick

Notice James says, "The prayer of faith." It is not just that we pray. We must pray in faith! Consider Hebrews 11:6: "And without faith it is impossible to please him, for whoever would draw near to God must believe that he exists and that he rewards those who seek him." With this Biblical view, we can then understand that faith is the power behind prayer.

So when you pray, are you praying with faith or are you praying with an attitude of "Maybe God will help me or maybe He won't." That type of roll-the-dice praying is not Biblical nor God glorifying.

It is unfortunate that James 5 has been hijacked by various groups. Some will argue that if you have an illness, it must mean there is sin in your life, or if you had more faith, you would experience divine healing. Neither are true.

Jesus shows us in John 9 that physical ailments are not always a result of direct, personal sin. The disciples thought that the blind man's parents had sinned, causing his physical blindness. Jesus taught us he was blind to display the glory of God!

Those pastors who say that you must have more faith to be healed, I often wonder what they do with the Scripture that Jesus taught in Matthew 17:20 that says, "...Because of your little faith. For truly, I say to you, if you have faith like a grain of mustard seed, you will say to this mountain, 'Move from here to there,' and it will move, and nothing will be impossible for you."

Jesus was teaching us that it is not the size of our faith that ultimately matters, because our faith only needs to be the size of a mustard seed. Rather, where our faith is directed determines the outcome. Jesus told us to have "...Faith in God" in Mark 11:22.

Sin and Sickness

As Christ followers, how are we to pray concerning sickness? We understand that sickness is a direct result of sin entering the world at the Garden of Eden. The reason sickness is not a part of heaven is because sin is not a part of heaven. While I believe Scripture teaches a direct link between sin and sickness, I do not believe that sickness is a personal punishment from God, as some people teach. As mentioned earlier, the blind man in John 9 shows us that his condition was not a result of sin.

I do think, however, that sickness is on the earth as a result of man's sin. So, should a believer experience an illness, I do not think that means the individual believer has sinned, but rather, it is a result of the sin upon humanity.

The question is this, how should Christians pray toward sickness? The answer is to follow the Biblical pattern of James 5. We confess sin, we call for the leadership of the church, we anoint with oil (symbolizing the Holy Spirit, inviting His help and guidance), and we pray fervent prayers of faith.

The Effects of Prayer and Confession

James 5:16 begins with the word, "Therefore." This is a transition word used many times in the New Testament. If you notice how it is used, the word *therefore* beautifully ties one promise to another.

So James says, "Therefore, confess your sins to one another and pray for one another." Why? Because in verse 15, God promises to work on our behalf! Note verse 15 says, "And the prayer of faith will save the one who is sick, and the Lord will raise him up. And if he has committed sins, he will be forgiven." Based on those promises, the word *therefore* is the conclusion that we should confess our sins to one another and pray for one another because of God's promise to actively work in our lives.

Note the progression. First we are to confess our sins to one another. Like all things in Scripture, there is a balance to find. Suppose a couple is having a rough time in their marriage where mistakes are being made. That couple should not air their dirty laundry to friends and others. Perhaps they talk to a pastor or counselor, but this is not saying that one spouse should share private details with others outside of that counseling. That would be more gossip and slander than confession of sins...especially if it is the sins of their spouse!

Rather, I think this confession should be to the one you have offended. So if I know that I have sinned against someone, I am to go to that person and confess what I know I have done to them. Jesus taught this principle in Matthew 5:23-24.

The word *confess* means to agree with. So if I am going confess my sin to God as well as the one I have offended, then it means I have to agree that I have committed a wrong action. Confession is an outward sign of inward repentance. When I am able to agree that my wrong has offended both God and others, then I can receive the wonderful forgiveness promised in 1 John 1:9, "If we confess our sins, he is faithful and just to forgive us our sins and to cleanse us from all unrighteousness."

Another advantage of confessing our sins to one another is creating accountability. If a man is struggling with lust and he is able to confide in and confess to a friend, that friend can begin to keep him accountable. Notice the next phrase of James 5:16, "And pray for one another." This is the beauty of a church family. I cannot pray for you effectively if I do not know you are struggling, nor can you pray for me if you are not aware of my struggles.

James 5 indicates that when we confess our sins to one another and are praying for one another, the outcome of this will be "that you may be healed." Whether this is a physical healing, spiritual healing, or emotional healing, there is certainly a healing that comes from the Lord when our sins are forgiven and our hearts are right before God and others.

Elijah, an Old Testament Example

James is going to help us understand how effective our prayers can be when he uses the Old Testament example of Elijah. While he is considered a spiritual giant, it is interesting that he also battled depression. Do you remember how he asked the Lord to take his life, even after seeing a major victory on Mount Carmel and defeating the prophets of Baal?

The point James is making with Elijah is that God was willing to use his prayers when, in fact, he was quite flawed. He struggled with doubts and fears just as we do at times. 1 Kings 19 shows us that after the miracle of calling down fire at Mount Carmel, Elijah ran in fear from Jezebel and Ahab. He immediately went into hiding and asked the Lord to take his life. He went into a deep depression after an incredible triumph.

So when James used an illustration about the effectiveness of prayer, he chose someone with very real flaws. I appreciate how the Bible shows us the mistakes of God's people. Not only does it help us avoid the same errors, but it is also a great comfort to know that God uses and helps those who do not have it all together! It shows me there is hope for my own life.

Do not let the devil convince you that you do not have the ability to pray effectively. If you do not have a burden for your loved ones and cry out to the Lord on their behalf, who will? No wonder Satan will try to discourage us. It is you that has the greatest responsibility to bring them before the Lord in prayer.

Fervent Praying

I've often asked the Lord why fervent prayer matters to Him. In my mind, it seems if God is going to answer the prayer, He will do it whether I pray fervently or not. So it intrigues me that the Bible seems to encourage fervent praying.

I have also struggled with the concept of fervent praying because, in a sense, it can seem like works to me. If my prayer is depending on how well or intensely I pray, then is that not works on my part? Is my faith in the God who answers prayer or in the way I am praying? I have seen so many try to manipulate God in the way they pray. I do not want to approach God in that kind of attitude.

One day the Lord spoke to my heart. It seemed he asked me, "When is your marriage at its best?" After thinking about it, I responded to the Lord, "When I put a lot into it." I knew then the Lord was showing me why fervent praying matters. The more I put into the prayer, the more I'm going to get out of it. The more I put into time with the Lord, the more blessing, the more faith, the more of Him I am going to have.

I think the reason God wants fervent praying is because we put much more into those prayers. We put more heart, more faith, more passion, and more hope into fervent praying. Did He not tell the Church of Laodicea in Revelation 3 that He would rather them be cold or hot rather than lukewarm? I have to ask myself how often I am lukewarm in my praying rather than fervent and passionate.

While I continue to seek the Lord and learn more about the subject of fervent praying, I am able to testify that it has been effective in my own life. There have been times I have cried out to the Lord, and I know God has heard and responded to the intensity with which I prayed.

Praying Loved One's Back to the Lord

To end chapter 5, it appears that James shifts gears to a different topic, but I do not believe he is changing the subject. I think he is still teaching us about prayer. He shifts in verses 19 and 20 by saying, "My brothers, if anyone among you wanders from the truth and someone brings him back, let him know that whoever brings back a sinner from his wandering will save his soul from death and will cover a multitude of sins."

I think James is encouraging us to intercede for lost loved ones. If someone falls away or goes into error, it is our effectual, fervent prayers that can bring them back to the Lord. It can get discouraging when you have prayed for someone and you have yet to see a change. But do not lose heart! These Scriptures are telling us to continue praying our loved ones back to the Lord. Be encouraged by a powerful thought E.M. Bounds shared back during the Civil War days. He wrote, "Prayers are deathless. The lips that uttered them may be closed in death, the heart that felt them may have ceased to beat, but the prayers live before God, and God's heart is set on them and prayers outlive the lives of those who uttered them; outlive a generation, outlive an age, outlive a world... Fortunate are they whose fathers and mothers have left them a wealthy patrimony of prayer."

I hope you will be encouraged to pray as never before. If you are someone who has prayed for quite a while and you are growing discouraged, I encourage you to dig in and pray all the more. Those prayers are working and they have great power to them. Read James 5 often and continue to call on the name of the Lord.

Chapter Thirteen
Satisfied in God

"Jesus said to them, 'My food is to do the will of him who sent me and to accomplish his work'" (John 4:34).

People who can pray effectively are not those who think they are super spiritual. It is not people who think they have mastered the art of praying nor are they the ones who spend large amounts of time in prayer. As we have learned in the chapters of this book, God does not measure our praying by any of these standards. Instead, the people who know how to get ahold of God are those who feel their deep need for Jesus.

It is when our hearts long for Him more than worldly comforts or personal agendas that we can really call on His name. When our desperation is at its greatest, we find ourselves nearest to the Savior.

If you want to grow deeper in prayer, the key is to get hungry. When you hunger for God's will, and you are hungry for His presence and His blessings, that is when you will begin to pray differently and pray effectively. However, if you are satisfied and content you will not discover the blessing of spiritual hunger.

Jesus taught in John 4:34 that His food was to do the will of God. This explains His drive and laser focus throughout His life and ministry. We never see Christ getting sidetracked. What we see is Jesus praying in the mornings, in the afternoons, and sometimes all night. His hunger was to accomplish what the Father had sent Him to do.

Can you and I say that we have the same type of hunger as Christ? I am at my best spiritually when I am focused on doing the will of God in my life. When I get off track and get wrapped up in doing what I want in life, I get spiritually weak.

What does food do for us physically? First, it strengthens us. People who do not eat are weak. It is usually a sign of illness when someone loses their appetite. When you eat a healthy, nutritious meal, you can feel its effects as it strengthens you. In a similar way, when you discover the will of God and begin to do it, that is when you feel strong. I see Christians all the time who are incredibly weak. Oh, they are healthy on the outside, but they are very weak in their spirit man.

Second, food sustains us. When we pray and strive to do God's will in our lives, we find it sustains us. Have you ever felt like giving up in the midst of a fierce trial? What is it that keeps you going? It is doing the will of God. Have you been so weak that you can hardly trust God? Those can be scary moments in our faith. We have seen multiple examples of people who looked to the Lord in the chapters of this book. When you face seasons of great weakness, know that it is doing the will of God that will give you strength over time. If you are about to give up as you read this, be encouraged and stay the course and continue the race, looking unto Jesus (Hebrews 12:2).

Lastly, food satisfies us. Do you know what it is to be satisfied by the Lord? I am talking about a satisfaction that you can feel deep in your soul. I am glad that I have gone through seasons where I learned firsthand what it meant to be satisfied by God.

One of the scariest seasons of my life was 2005-2006. I felt very dissatisfied with ministry and with life. It was my greatest season of struggle. The Lord helped me through this time period. He gave me a song that meant so much to me. It is a familiar song to many, but for me, it was a like a well in a desert. It is called "Fill my cup." The lyrics read,

"Fill my cup, Lord. I lift it up, Lord. Come and quench this thirsting of my soul. Bread of Heaven, Feed me till I want no more. Here's my cup, fill it up and make me whole."

I would sing that in my heart over and over. It strengthened, sustained, and satisfied me. When I hear it now, my mind goes back to the times that God would minister to my heart through its sweet melody and trusting words.

If you feel weak, restless, or dissatisfied, ask yourself if you are hungry to accomplish the will of God? Throughout 2005 and 2006, I found the Lord faithful when I cried out to Him. He quenched my thirsts. He satisfied me. It is a testimony of God's goodness, and I know that you will find Him just as faithful in your own spiritual walk.

Ponder and pray over Psalm 63:1-4, "O God, you are my God; earnestly I seek you; my soul thirsts for you; my flesh faints for you, as in a dry and weary land where there is no water. So I have looked upon you in the sanctuary, beholding your power and glory. Because your steadfast love is better than life, my lips will praise you. So I will bless you as long as I live; in your name I will lift up my hands."

God can quench your thirsts. If God's love is better than life, then surely His love is better than anything this life has to offer. Find yourself strengthened, sustained, and satisfied in Christ alone.

Epilogue

Our lives are a series of hills and valleys, joys and sorrows, gains and losses. Since I first penned *Calling on the Name of the Lord*, my life has taken many different twists and turns. One could look at my life and say I have suffered a great deal of loss. But if you look at my life in the spiritual sense, I see nothing but gain. I began this book telling the story of my dad's terminal illness. Since its first publication, so many have asked me about my dad, so I wanted to close with an epilogue of my dad's story. On January 3, 2017, my dad's faith became sight. He departed this earth with all of its pain, sorrow, and sin. He then stepped onto the shores of heaven with all of its joys and beauty, and with Christ Himself. The Lord ministered so wonderfully to me during the time of my dad's passing. He showed me Psalm 116:15, "Precious in the eyes of the Lord is the death of his saints." The Lord showed me that if my dad's death was precious in the eyes of God, then his death would become precious in my eyes as well. I did grieve my dad's death but, as Paul reminds us, we do not grieve as those who have no hope (1 Thessalonians 4:13). Grieving is different for a Christian. Randy Alcorn reminds us that just because someone has passed away, that does not mean they cease to exist. So often we say we're sorry for someone's loss, but the reality is I have not lost my dad. I know exactly where he is. He is in the presence of the Lord (Jude 1:24). The Bible assures us to be absent from the body is to be present with the Lord (2 Corinthians 5:8).

CS Lewis wonderfully stated, "We are not a body that has a soul. Instead, we are a soul that happens to have a body." It is our soul that is created in the image of God. When this tent, as the great apostle Paul calls it, wears out and gives way, then our soul goes to be with the Lord (2 Corinthians 5:1). This is why my confidence is so strong in what Jesus said, that if anyone believes in him, though he dies, yet shall he live (John 11:25). So while in human terms my dad's death seems as though it was a great loss, the Bible calls it a great gain. Read Philippians 1:21, "For me to live is Christ, but to die is gain." I had that written on my dad's headstone. What has my father gained by going to heaven? Well, he gained all that heaven holds. He gained all the joy of heaven. He gained all the benefits of heaven and most of all he has gained Christ Himself, the hope of our salvation.

The Lord gave my family two other great things after the loss of my dad. He gave us our two sons, Hudson Graham and John Mark, born in the midst of all of this. The line in John Newton's song "Amazing Grace" that says "through many dangers, toils, and snares we have already come" has become very personal to me. In 2017, following my dad's passing, I quickly began losing my eyesight. I faced two major eye surgeries that failed and detached the retina in my left eye, leaving me permanently blind in that eye. In a little over a year, I would lose complete eyesight in my right eye as well. I lost all eyesight in November 2018, shortly before the birth of our last son. As you can imagine, this left me reeling and asking many questions. What kind of husband and father would I be? Could I continue to pastor my church? Would I even be able to continue preaching if I could not read and study? Knowing that blindness was coming, I began to try to prepare myself as best as I could emotionally, physically, and spiritually. The Lord promised me that his grace would be sufficient for me. But as you know, there are some things we just cannot know until we face them.

Prior to blindness, I was a type-A personality, a workaholic, and did not adapt well to change. Even though there were many difficult days, the Lord helped me to adapt quickly. I was surprised how my other senses kicked into high gear. My sense of touch, smell, and especially hearing improved dramatically. My wife is always amazed at how well I can hear. I was surprised at how quickly my children adapted to this new disability. I still play with them, wrestle, joke, and prank with them, and especially pray with them. Most of all, I was surprised at the power of God that came on my preaching. I was afraid that many people would leave my church now that it had a blind pastor. In reality, it has been the exact opposite. Our church has grown by leaps and bounds, both in faith and in numbers. Rather than taking a step back in preaching, God has enabled me to take great steps forward. In the midst of blindness, God's grace has been sufficient.

Even more evidence that God was leading me into this season of blindness was when He spoke to me to stop preaching with notes half a year before I started losing eyesight. I had begun a series on the book of Acts in January 2017. A few weeks into that series, I felt the Holy Spirit tell me that He wanted me to depend more on the Holy Spirit in my preaching than on my sermon notes. I was still to prepare my sermons aggressively, but the Lord did not want me to speak using notes. Little did I know that by that summer, the process of losing vision would begin. It gives me confidence that God saw this coming and prepared me before the trial came to my life.

Going into blindness, I knew the Lord would be faithful, but I never dreamed this season would prove to be this fruitful. I knew His grace would sustain me, but I never imagined just how sustaining it would be. The last time I drove a vehicle was the final Sunday of October in 2018. I thought that would be one of the hardest aspects of being blind, losing mobility, not having the freedom to just jump in my car and go wherever I wished. Friends, I say this as transparently as I possibly can—I have not had one urge to drive since I went blind. I call that the grace of God in action.

Today I live in a new rhythm, in what I call a pace of grace. Every meal I enjoy with my family, every sermon I prepare and preach, every marriage I counsel, every book, music CD, podcast, and sermon series I create, I do so by the sheer grace of God. Again, some would say I have suffered so much loss but no, my friend, there is much I have gained. God has now given me the fruits of self-control and patience. God has given me more contentment than I ever thought was possible. But most of all, God has given me His rich grace to the point I can say I have tasted and seen that the Lord is good (Psalm 34:8).

A Word to the Reader

Preaching Christ Church is dedicated to creating resources that encourage people in their walk with Christ. By visiting our website, you can discover sermons, video teachings, devotionals, articles and podcasts that will help you grow in Christ.

Discover more at *www.preachingchristchurch.com or www.awakenedtograce.com*

Download Our FREE Mobile App: Awakened To Grace

When you download the Awakened to Grace App, you will enjoy On-Demand access to Sermons (Video & Audio), Inspiring Music, Engaging Podcast and much more. Awakened to Grace is the teaching ministry of Pastor Chad Roberts and Preaching Christ Church.

Discover more at
www.awakenedtograce.com

Other Books by Pastor Chad

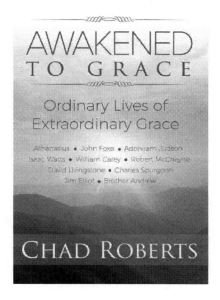

Order *Awakened To Grace: Ordinary Lives of Extraordinary Grace* through Amazon.com or ChadRobertsBooks.com

ISBN: 1542761409
Paperback Edition: $12.99

Other Books by Pastor Chad

Order *He's in the Waiting: 30 Readings to Help You Wait on God* through Amazon.com or ChadRobertsBooks.com

ISBN: 1722490292
Paperback Edition: $12.99

Music From
Awakened To Grace

Stream All of our Music on our Free Mobile App: Awakened
To Grace

If you would like a physical copy you can order at
www.awakenedtograce.com

Preaching Christ Church

Preaching Christ Church is located in Kingsport, TN. It was planted by Pastor Chad in 2001 with less than 10 people. Since then, it has grown into a healthy and vibrant congregation that exists to glorify God by spreading the Gospel of Jesus Christ.

Learn more about PCC by visiting,
www.preachingchristchurch.com